**GENERAL EDITOR: JAMES GIBSO**

JA:

.ond Wilson
..... Richard Wirdnam
SA:
*Waiting for Godot* Jennifer Birkett
WI_____ TH

RO                                                              l Smith
CH.ARLC
EMILY E                                                         ear
JOHN BU                                                         e Batson
GEOFFE                                                          ander
                                                                Lester
                                                                as Marsh
                                                                n
                                                                *Tales*
                                                                an
JOSEPH                                                          ne
CHARL

                                                                tts
GEORC                                                           y

                                                                heeler
T. S. EL                                                        _apworth
                                                                rick
HENRY                                                           on
E. M. F

                                                                pear
WILLI/
                                                                ilson
OLIVE                                                           anger
THOM                                                            ay Evans
                                                                s Gibson
*Far from the Madding Crowd* Colin
Temblett-Wood

BEN JONSON            *Volpone*  Michael Stout
JOHN KEATS           *Selected Poems*  John Garrett
RUDYARD KIPLING      *Kim*  Leonée Ormond

# MACMILLAN MASTER GUIDES

| | |
|---|---|
| PHILIP LARKIN | *The Whitsun Weddings* and *The Less Deceived*   Andrew Swarbrick |
| D. H. LAWRENCE | *Sons and Lovers*   R. P. Draper |
| HARPER LEE | *To Kill a Mockingbird*   Jean Armstrong |
| LAURIE LEE | *Cider with Rosie*   Brian Tarbitt |
| GERARD MANLEY HOPKINS | *Selected Poems*   R. J. C. Watt |
| CHRISTOPHER MARLOWE | *Doctor Faustus*   David A. Male |
| THE METAPHYSICAL POETS | Joan van Emden |
| THOMAS MIDDLETON and WILLIAM ROWLEY | *The Changeling*   Tony Bromham |
| ARTHUR MILLER | *The Crucible*   Leonard Smith<br>*Death of a Salesman*   Peter Spalding |
| GEORGE ORWELL | *Animal Farm*   Jean Armstrong |
| WILLIAM SHAKESPEARE | *Richard II*   Charles Barber<br>*Othello*   Tony Bromham<br>*Hamlet*   Jean Brooks<br>*King Lear*   Francis Casey<br>*Henry V*   Peter Davison<br>*The Winter's Tale*   Diana Devlin<br>*Julius Caesar*   David Elloway<br>*Macbeth*   David Elloway<br>*The Merchant of Venice*   A. M. Kinghorn<br>*Measure for Measure*   Mark Lilly<br>*Henry IV Part I*   Helen Morris<br>*Romeo and Juliet*   Helen Morris<br>*A Midsummer Night's Dream*   Kenneth Pickering<br>*The Tempest*   Kenneth Pickering<br>*Coriolanus*   Gordon Williams<br>*Antony and Cleopatra*   Martin Wine |
| GEORGE BERNARD SHAW | *St Joan*   Leonée Ormond |
| RICHARD SHERIDAN | *The School for Scandal*   Paul Ranger<br>*The Rivals*   Jeremy Rowe |
| ALFRED TENNYSON | *In Memoriam*   Richard Gill |
| EDWARD THOMAS | *Selected Poems*   Gerald Roberts |
| ANTHONY TROLLOPE | *Barchester Towers*   K. M. Newton |
| JOHN WEBSTER | *The White Devil* and *The Duchess of Malfi*   David A. Male |
| VIRGINIA WOOLF | *To the Lighthouse*   John Mepham<br>*Mrs Dalloway*   Julian Pattison |
| WILLIAM WORDSWORTH | *The Prelude Books I and II*   Helen Wheeler |

# MACMILLAN MASTER GUIDES
# THE PILGRIM'S PROGRESS
# BY JOHN BUNYAN

BEATRICE BATSON

## M
## MACMILLAN
## EDUCATION

First edition 1988

Published by
MACMILLAN EDUCATION LTD
Houndmills, Basingstoke, Hampshire RG2 2XS
and London
Companies and representatives
throughout the world

Printed in Hong Kong

British Library Cataloguing in Publication Data
Batson, Beatrice
The pilgrim's progress by John Bunyan.—
(Macmillan master guides).
1. Bunyan, John. Pilgrim's Progress
I. Title   II. Bunyan, John. Pilgrim's Progress
823′.4     PR3330.A95
ISBN 0–333–43687–3 Pbk
ISBN 0–333–43688–1 Pbk export

# CONTENTS

# GENERAL EDITOR'S PREFACE

The aim of the Macmillan Master Guides is to help you to appreciate the book you are studying by providing information about it and by suggesting ways of reading and thinking about it which will lead to a fuller understanding. The section on the writer's life and background has been designed to illustrate those aspects of the writer's life which have influenced the work, and to place it in its personal and literary context. The summaries and critical commentary are of special importance in that each brief summary of the action is followed by an examination of the significant critical points. The space which might have been given to repetitive explanatory notes has been devoted to a detailed analysis of the kind of passage which might confront you in an examination. Literary criticism is concerned with both the broader aspects of the work being studied and with its detail. The ideas which meet us in reading a great work of literature, and their relevance to us today, are an essential part of our study, and our Guides look at the thought of their subject in some detail. But just as essential is the craft with which the writer has constructed his work of art, and this may be considered under several technical headings – characterisation, language, style and stagecraft, for example.

The authors of these Guides are all teachers and writers of wide experience, and they have chosen to write about books they admire and know well in the belief that they can communicate their admiration to you. But you yourself must read and know intimately the book you are studying. No one can do that for you. You should see this book as a lamp-post. Use it to shed light, not to lean against. If you know your text and know what it is saying about life, and how it says it, then you will enjoy it, and there is no better way of passing an examination in literature.

JAMES GIBSON

# ACKNOWLEDGEMENTS

In my quotations from *The Pilgrim's Progress* I have used the edition prepared by N. H. Keeble, published by Oxford University Press. This book is listed among the primary sources which I recommend in the Further Reading section.

I should like to thank the staff of the British Library, the Newberry Library of Chicago, and the Wheaton College Library for their ready assistance in numerous ways. My thanks also go to the Curator of the Bunyan Museum, Bedford, for showing me the collection of Bunyan memorabilia, a reminder of the creative energy of the tinker, preacher and writer.

My deep appreciation goes to Croom Helm Ltd, publisher of my book, *Allegory and Imagination*, for permitting me to quote occasional lines from that work. To Yvonne Robery, Secretary of the Department of English at Wheaton College, I offer my sincere gratitude for giving unstintingly of her time to prepare the typescript.

BEATRICE BATSON

Cover illustration: *Christian Reading in His Book* by William Blake © The Frick Collection, New York.

*For my sisters and brothers*

# 1 JOHN BUNYAN: THE MAN, PREACHER AND AUTHOR

John Bunyan (1628–88) was born at Elstow, near Bedford, England, the oldest son of a tinker. Although he speaks in his autobiography of his father's family as 'being of that rank that is meanest and most despised of all the families in the land', his family had once been landed yeomen. Emphasis on his humble birth is hardly inverted snobbery; it is Bunyan's way of attributing solely to God credit for what he had become. His education was undoubtedly slight. The only information on the subject is his own statement: 'Notwithstanding the meanness and inconsiderableness of my parents, it pleased God to put it into their heart, to put me to school.' If he did attend school, which may have been the grammar school at Bedford or the one in the neighbouring parish of Houghton Conquest, it seems that it was for only a short period. The year 1644 was a year of bereavement and adjustment for Bunyan. His mother died in June; his younger sister, Margaret, died in July, and his father married for the third time in August. In November he was summoned in a county levy for service in the Parliamentary Army, which opposed the Royalists (those who supported the King and the official Church of England) during the civil war which had broken out in England in 1642.

What active service Bunyan knew is uncertain; no significant battles were fought near Newport Pagnell, where he was stationed, and Bunyan makes no reference to any specific military engagements. In 1647 he volunteered for service in Ireland and was about to embark when his regiment was disbanded; consequently, he probably saw little or no active service. He returned to Elstow and continued to work as a tinker.

Bunyan was a lover of music but had little money with which to buy instruments. This failed to hamper him: he hammered a violin out of iron and later carved a flute from one of the legs of a four-legged stool, which was among his sparse furnishings in a prison cell where he spent twelve years.

He was married twice. His first wife, a person as poor as he, brought him a simple dowry of two well-known Puritan works, Arthur Dent's *The Plain Man's Path-way to Heaven* and Lewis Bayly's *The Practice of Piety*. What the name of his first wife was, history failed to record. Four children were born to this marriage, including a blind daughter, Mary. His second wife, Elizabeth, was a magnificently brave woman who stood in the face of hostility from the powerful and pleaded the cause of John Bunyan, especially when she feared he would be sentenced to prison for his preaching. Elizabeth and John Bunyan had three children.

Bunyan etches his spiritual progress in a series of imperishable vignettes. What characterises many depictions is a series of crises. One of the earliest pictures is his being interrupted in the midst of a game of tipcat by a voice from heaven which calls on him to leave his sins. To the amazement of onlookers he stands transfixed as he considers the alternatives before him, but following the brief pause he continues with the game. This action typifies the visual method of his prolonged crisis: moving back and forth between an external occurrence and an internal struggle associated with it.

The most vivid source of various vignettes is his spiritual autobiography, *Grace Abounding*, published in 1666. The first part of the autobiography pinpoints his youthful sins and God's care of him; it moves on with his reaction to numerous temptations, especially analysing his doubts regarding his being among the elect (those specially chosen by God for Salvation). The climax comes when Bunyan believes that he is yielding to a startling temptation to 'sell' Christ. Following this crisis, the autobiography explores his struggles as he suffers not only the sense of common human sin but also deep personal guilt. The climax of this section is reached in a dramatic portrayal of Bunyan's vision of God and Christ: a scene of redemption.

Bunyan's first discovery of what Christian fellowship might mean comes when he overhears 'three or four poor women sitting at a door in the room, and talking about the things of God'. Later he remarks: 'I thought they spoke as if joy did make them speak; they spoke with such pleasantness of Scriptural language and with such appearance of grace in all they said, that they were to me as if they had found a new world . . . .' Step by step, he found himself drawn into the fellowship of which these poor women were a part.

A few years prior to 1654, Bunyan met and received counsel from John Gifford, minister of the open communion Baptist Church at Bedford. In 1654, he joined Gifford's church. He moved from Elstow to Bedford and began to preach in villages near Bedford. His preaching coincided with the Restoration of King Charles II in 1660, frequently called the Stuart Restoration. The new government took harsh measures against the Nonconformists – those churches and religious groups which stood against the official Church of England. Bunyan was one of the first Nonconformists to experience the imposition of new restrictions under Charles II. Preaching unauthorised by the official Church was a punishable offence. Thus, in November, 1660, as he was preparing to begin a service in a village near Bedford, Bunyan was arrested for holding a conventicle (an illegal religious meeting), and 'for not conforming to the national worship of the Church of England'. He was sentenced in January 1661, initially for three months, to imprisonment in Bedford jail. His continued refusal to assure the authorities that he would refrain from preaching if released, prolonged his imprisonment until 1672. During these years the authorities granted him occasional time out of prison, and church records show that he attended several meetings at the Bedford Church. While in prison, he made shoe-laces in order to support his family, preached to prisoners, and wrote various works.

Bunyan's first prison book was *Profitable Meditations*, followed by *Christian Behaviour*, *The Holy City* and *Grace Abounding*. From 1667 to 1672 he probably spent most of his time writing *The Pilgrim's Progress*. This book, published in 1678, was for generations the work, next to the Bible, most deeply cherished in devout English-speaking homes. When the great missionary surge began, Protestants translated into various dialects first the Bible, then *The Pilgrim's Progress*.

On 21 January 1672, the Bedford congregation called John Bunyan to be pastor. In March he was released from prison – even though he spent six additional months in jail in 1677 – and on 9 May, he was licensed to preach under Charles II's Declaration of Indulgence. During the same year the Bedford church became licensed as a Congregational meeting place.

Bunyan's dedication, diligence and zeal as preacher, evangelist and pastor earned him the nickname of 'Bishop Bunyan'. Although he frequently preached in villages near Bedford, and at times in London churches, he always refused to make his home away from Bedford.

Combined with his preaching and pastoral responsibilities was a heavy schedule of writing. Following the publication of *The Pilgrim's Progress* (Part One), there appeared *The Life and Death of Mr Badman* (1680) and *The Holy War* (1682), an allegory of the struggle between the forces of Good and Evil for man's soul. *The Second Part of The Pilgrim's Progress* was published in 1684. Here the emphasis is on the Christian community rather than on the embattled figure of Part One. The second part is also less dangerous and consequently a more relaxed journey. His last book – he wrote more than sixty, including his sermons – was called *A Book for Boys and Girls*, published in 1686.

Journeying to London to deliver a sermon, Bunyan rode out of his way to Reading, to assist in bringing reconciliation between a father and son. He then left to ride the forty miles to London. As a result of the heavy rains he encountered, he contracted a fever. On 31 August 1688 he died at the home of his London friend, John Strudwick and was buried in Bunhill Fields.

# 2 THE RELIGIOUS BACKGROUND

## 2.1 PURITANISM

John Bunyan's life story is usually associated with Puritanism, a term
frequently misunderstood. Puritanism can hardly be categorised as a
rigid system of ideas with a clearly-defined historical origin. It has no
founder, and no specific date marks its beginning. It might more
accurately be called a way of life or a characteristic spirit of certain
Christian believers. Without question, *The Pilgrim's Progress* is one
of the chief avenues by which this Puritan spirit entered the main-
stream of English tradition.

Puritanism, a feature of the Protestant Reformation in England,
first assumed the form of an organised movement in the 1560s during
the reign of Queen Elizabeth I. Characteristics of the Puritan spirit,
which we shall later examine, indicate, however, that its roots reach
back into preceding centuries. Roger Sharrock holds that the Lol-
lards, followers of the well-trained scholar and religious leader, John
Wycliffe, who were active in the East Midlands of England during the
late fourteenth and early fifteenth centuries, anticipated the Puritan
lay preachers. Wycliffe himself had denounced the priestly system of
the Church. The Puritanism of the seventeenth century, however, in
a more specialised sense began as a specific Church movement during
the reign of Elizabeth I. The Queen established within the Church of
England the Elizabethan Compromise which sought to merge Calvinistic doctrine, a Catholic worship, and episcopal church government.

The tenets of Calvinistic doctrine appealed to the Puritans and
served as the foundation of their faith. These tenets included: the
depravity of man, the sovereignty of God, salvation by faith in Christ,

God's election of individuals to salvation, the irresistibility of God's grace, and the centrality of the Bible in belief and in life. The Puritans were displeased, however, with Church hierarchy and what they considered to be the remaining vestiges of the Catholic ritual in worship. To purify the Church from within, not of its doctrine, but of its ritualistic ceremony and hierarchical structure, was the desire of many Puritans; others believed it to be impossible to conform to the Established Church. As the seventeenth century wore on, many Puritans became separatists or nonconformists.

Puritans did not, however, focus only on correct theology or on worship and church government. Their primary concern was the application of God's providence to every area of personal life. Contrary to the pejorative sense in which Puritans are often viewed, they did not conceive of a holy life by negative standards or solely in terms of abstinence or asceticism. It is true that they practised and lived their faith with an intensity rarely known in our day, but this heightened rather than hampered their enjoyment.

One eminent Puritan preacher held that amusements and lawful games were refreshing both to mind and body and should be encouraged. Although they opposed bear-baiting, cock-fighting and the like, the Puritans did so because they believed that these forms of recreation were often associated with gambling and brutality. Eating, drinking, singing and dancing are celebrated over and over in *The Pilgrim's Progress*, and these enjoyments were gifts from God. No celebration, however, should violate Sunday. This day was holy and sacred, and Puritans condemned its not being observed as such. Games were forbidden, and the day was to be spent in rest and worship. In the words of Richard Baxter, a Puritan author, Sunday should be spent 'in hearing the Word of God truly preached, thereby to learn and to do His will; in receiving the sacraments rightly administered; in using public and private prayer; in collection for the poor and in doing of good works; and chiefly in the true obedience of the inward man'. Sunday was sometimes called 'the market day of the soul', a day to do business with God. Rest and religious meditation were central to the Puritan idea of honouring Sunday.

To the Puritans there was no dichotomy between responding to the good things of life and believing that life was a warfare against sin. They believed that every facet of human experience should be motivated by a dynamic Christianity. Self-discipline preceded by self-examination was extremely important, for the unexamined life was not worth living. Life had purpose: God gave every individual a calling and the talents or gifts to follow that calling in honour, and under the scrutiny, of God. They had no piecemeal view of life: there was no sacred and secular, only obedience and disobedience, and all vocations were holy callings.

If the Puritans were responsive to life's enjoyments and were concerned with their behaviour and purpose in the world, so also were they interested in intellectual pursuits. They held that the new science of the seventeenth century and its theories, as well as humanistic philosophies, should be explored and examined. For many Puritans their intellectual inclination also embodied a love of beauty and art. Furthermore, their appreciation for beauty extended to creation and to creatures in the world. In various sermons, Bunyan referred feelingly to the toils of the spider, the work of a hive of bees, the beauty of the sun, moon and stars, the glory of the rainbow, the song of the birds, the order of flowers in an English garden and the habits of beasts of the fields. To neglect the beauty in creation, Bunyan indicated, was to ignore manifestations of God Himself.

## 2.2 THE 'PARTICULAR BAPTISTS'

It should probably be noted that, although Bunyan is generally referred to as a Puritan, he was never among those who sought to purify the Anglican or the Established Church. It is equally true that he preferred a simple form of worship with emphasis on the centrality of the Bible, rather than on liturgical form. He is widely referred to as a 'Particular Open Communion Baptist', one of a separatist group distinctly known for being broad-minded about various methods of baptism and about church membership. However, to label Bunyan as any particular separatist presents problems.

In several of his writings Bunyan calls attention to the stupidity of those who give more attention to labels and doctrinal minutiae than to the grace that can lead individuals to God. In his work, *A Holy Life*, Bunyan states:

It is strange to see at this day how, notwithstanding all the threatenings of God, men are wedded to their own opinions, beyond what the law of grace and love will admit. Here is a Presbyter, here is an Independent, and a Baptist, so joined each man to his own opinion, that they cannot have that communion one with another, as by the testimony of The Lord Jesus they are commanded and enjoined.

## 2.3  CONTROVERSY BETWEEN BUNYAN AND THE QUAKERS

Despite his aversion to bickering, however, Bunyan entered into controversy with individuals of other religions. His first book, *Some Gospel Truths Opened* (1656) was directed against the Quakers, followers of the religious leader, George Fox, who believed that Christianity was not an outward profession, but an inner light by which Christ directly illuminated the believing soul. Furthermore, revelation was not confined to the Scriptures; though the true Word of God, they were not the only way God spoke to people. Although the conflict with the Quakers appeared on the surface to be little more than professional rivalry, the differences were by no means simply petty jealousies for John Bunyan.

He deeply feared the Quakers' doctrine of the inner light and their treatment of Scripture. What Bunyan emphasised was a valid personal experience based on the teaching of Scripture. In his judgement, the Quaker doctrine of the 'inner light' lacked the objective character of special revelation.

If his controversy with the Quakers seemed acrimonious, and his second book, *A Vindication of Some Gospel Truths Opened* (1657), a reply to the equally acrimonious Edward Burrough, a Quaker leader, was surely somewhat passionate, there was also a positive aspect. Bunyan convincingly demonstrated with emotional interest his sincere and zealous belief in Scripture as the foundation for Christian belief.

## 2.4  CONTROVERSY BETWEEN BUNYAN AND THE ANGLICANS

If the Quaker doctrines troubled John Bunyan, so also did some of the teaching voiced by Anglican leaders. Edward Fowler, an Anglican divine, wrote a book called *Design of Christianity* (1670). He contended that the essence of Christianity lay in the perfecting of man's moral nature and in the restoration of lives to the perfect righteousness which they originally possessed in Adam. Although he was in prison at the time of the publication of Fowler's book, Bunyan obtained a copy and read it. To suggest as Fowler did that Christ simply restores man to his original righteousness was regarded by Bunyan as a threat to Christian doctrine of justification by the righteousness of Christ alone. In brief, Bunyan held that righteousness came only through God's putting on man the righteousness of God through Christ. The dialogue between Bunyan and Fowler continued until it became a series of diatribes. What constituted the essence of Bunyan's position is in his book, *A Defence of the Doctrine of Justification by Faith*, in which he attacked Fowler for his heretical theology and his 'unstable weathercock spirit'.

Prior to his fight with Fowler, Bunyan wrote a minor treatise, *I Will Pray with the Spirit* (1663), which was written against the set of forms of the *Book of Common Prayer*. The treatise lacked the pugnacious tone that permeated his exchange with Fowler. To express conviction in a variety of tones was not unique in the writings of John Bunyan. Referring to seventeenth-century writers, Anne Ferry spoke of these writers expressing 'passionate conviction' in tones 'not always solemn but often scornful, sarcastic, furious, playful, ironic, sophisticated, sweet' and in accents which 'seem indecorous, even irreverent'.

# 3 THE LITERARY
# BACKGROUND

Works of religious literature pervaded seventeenth-century England; the writer who concerned himself with religious doctrine, religious experience or religious institutions could be sure of engaging the attention of a vast range of readers. Writers assumed that their audiences were familiar with Scripture, had a thorough knowledge of Christian doctrine, and were faithful believers. These assumptions were made about the audiences not as professors and students in theology, but as ordinary citizens and Protestants. Although they demonstrated various temperaments, emphases, and genres in their writings, authors knew how to engage the attention of the audience on religious subjects.

## 3.1  THE SERMON AS A LITERARY TYPE

The well-constructed sermon was a source of extraordinary rhetorical power. Manuals on structuring a skilfully organised sermon were carefully studied by preachers of the seventeenth century. Sermons had to be structured in an orderly manner, but they also had to appeal to the wholeness of a person's being: the mind, the spirit and the imagination. What is especially enlightening for the student of literature is to observe analogies in which the nature of a religious experience is made clearer through its comparison to a more familiar ordinary experience. The writer may, for example, use such comparisons at different times to make clear the spiritual predicament of sinful man, to suggest the nature of God's work in redeeming man, and to exemplify some of the various aspects of the relationship between God and man.

The observation of analogies leads to the appropriation of the simile (the likening of a person or a thing to another). This literary feature, which Bunyan frequently uses, aids in keeping unconfused the person or thing and its likeness, or it fixes in the memory of the listener or reader the abstract argument through the analysis of a selected image.

In the sermon, *The Heavenly Footman*, for example, Bunyan chose the similitude of a race to be run. Basing his sermon on a Biblical text (I Corinthians 10:24), he analysed seven reasons for clarifying the image of the runner in the race, followed by nine directions on 'how to run so as to obtain' and nine motives for running the race. He next added nine 'uses' to determine whether or not the runners were in earnest about the race. He closed with an admonition to begin the race and stay in it until the end. By the close of the sermon, a reader should have no difficulty in fixing the image of the race to be run in the memory.

A tremendous array of similes from every facet of the natural world illumines spiritual matters for Bunyan. He remarks, for instance, 'Zeal without knowledge is like a nettled horse without eyes, or like a sword in a madman's hand', or 'Faith dissolves doubts as the sun drives away the mists'.

Since the authors of the seventeenth-century sermon find their dominant sources to be two books: the book of the Word (the Bible) and the book of the world (the world and the infinite variety of creatures in the world), it is no surprise that sermonisers, including Bunyan, find the world and its creatures to be rich sources for instruction. The glory of the sun, moon, and stars as well as the beauty of an English garden, manifest the majesty and beauty of God. The labour and toil of the ant and spider condemn sloth and idleness; the young ravens, depending upon God and loving their young, condemn liars and cheaters. John Donne, another great sermoniser and an outstanding poet of the seventeenth century, refers to these various objects of creation as a 'huge library' in which one reads of God. What Bunyan particularly believes is that the book of creatures may be read by any man. To neglect this book is to ignore manifestations of God as well as moral instruction in obedience, fruitfulness, wisdom, labour and love that the book of creatures embodies.

Analogies and similes are not the only features of the sermon as literary type. Other components include the metaphor, anecdotes, emblems, dialogue and rhetorical questions. At times Bunyan's handling of literary features shows a crudity not seen in sermons of the more formally trained preachers, but it is still a happy fact that he creates through them powerful effects.

## 3.2  THE SPIRITUAL AUTOBIOGRAPHY

During the seventeenth century the spiritual autobiography as an art form began to flourish in England. Proponents of various theological beliefs searched for religious understanding. They attempted to determine to what extent the Scriptures, the traditions of the Church, the Book of Nature, the promptings of the 'inner voice', and human reason could be trusted as valid guides. The belief that the individual could and should scrutinise the state of his spiritual welfare was an assumption shared by the Puritans and non-Puritans. The process and the resulting findings of such scrutiny became the source of one of the most popular genres of the period, the spiritual autobiography.

Between 1600 and 1640, spiritual autobiographies were written sporadically, three or four each decade. In the years between 1640 and 1660, the number doubled and doubled again from 1660 to 1670, continuing at that level until the close of the century. The popularity of the genre may be partially due to two factors: the presence of universal and recurrent features in the soul's experiences of all religious individuals, and similarities in religious experience which enabled individuals to measure their own growth.

Although there can be a strong relationship between religious doctrine and spiritual autobiography, the two genres must not be confused. Roy Pascal in his excellent book, *Design and Truth in Autobiography*, rightly contends that 'autobiography is not an appropriate means to urge the objective truth of a doctrine – though it may reveal more profound and general truths of life which the doctrine only partially formulates'. What Pascal suggests is that the spiritual autobiography is a literary form, and literature teaches by indirection, not through expository statements. Sally McFague, in *Speaking in Parables*, says that autobiography is 'a story of a life, and the best autobiographies are written precisely as a story, that is, as an ordering of events around a central focus'. The 'story' should not be confused with memoirs in which an author simply relates facts about his childhood, his ancestors, his education, his career, and other observable matters. Further, the 'story' should not be confused with diaries or journals, which depict with a minimal degree of selectivity, series of events in a life.

As a literary genre, then, autobiography unfolds the inner experiences and gives order and meaning to past experience from a present perspective. The primary thrust of the genre is to show *who* someone *is* or to reveal a map of the various inner experiences of an individual.

*Grace Abounding*, John Bunyan's spiritual autobiography, focuses on the inner self of Bunyan and shows him briefly as a child and then as a young man with a growing sensitivity to God. The self continues to unfold as he ponders the joys of some 'poor women' of Bedford, as he denies his 'carnal friends', as he begins to study the Bible, and as he fears that he may not be among those specially chosen by God for eternal life. The story of his life consists primarily of tensions between doubt and despair, joy and sorrow, love and fear, struggle and rest, and finally, with the relaxing of tension, a wonderful admiration for God and his wisdom. What is especially striking about *Grace Abounding* is the similarity between Bunyan's own spiritual conflicts and those of the hero of *The Pilgrim's Progress*.

## 3.3  ALLEGORY AS A LITERARY FORM

Bunyan wrote his most popular literary work, *The Pilgrim's Progress*, in the form of an allegory. It is wise to remember, however, that allegory as narrative began in the Middle Ages, the greatest being Dante Alighieri's (1265–1321) *The Divine Comedy*. The form was popular in medieval and Renaissance writing, but it is less popular in modern literature. Allegory is also less often found in short poems than in long works such as *Everyman*, *The Faerie Queen*, and *The Pilgrim's Progress*.

In recent years thinking about allegory has taken two main forms, emphasising, as Leopold Damrosch states, 'either the ability of its images to denote universal truths, or else insisting on their arbitrary nature'. Some thinkers of the modern era suggest that allegory appeals to us as readers of a 'system of signs'. What students may discover in Bunyan's allegory is the way in which his 'signs' point to an invisible world and, at the same time, to the allegorical nature of this world as an embodiment of meaning.

Exactly what allegory is remains a concern for some students and teachers. A brief look at a few views may help to clarify the concern and, at the same time, provide direction for reading an allegory. Some readers attempt to restrict allegory to a one-to-one correspondence. They suggest that more than one meaning is the province of the symbol, not allegory. It is more accurate to contend that allegory and the symbol are two ways of dealing with the 'fact' of a relationship between 'visible and invisible reality'. Allegory is hardly to be considered as only a disguised concept or idea but rather as a structure of images which releases various meanings. It is true that these various meanings have a tendency to be more fixed in allegory than in symbol.

A helpful way to see allegory is not exclusively as one comparison drawn out as in an extended metaphor, but rather to see the various figures and details as a series of related comparisons. A minor character, for example, such as Pliable in *The Pilgrim's Progress*, is surely pliable when he shows his eagerness to join Christian on his journey; he is equally pliable when he turns away from the journey; and after becoming a turncoat, he further shows himself to be pliable when he guiltily sneaks among his neighbours because of his behaviour. Although it is a structure of images, allegory differs from symbolism in that it tends to place less emphasis on the images as images and more on the ulterior meaning.

An intelligent way to define allegory in a simple manner is to consider it as a narrative that has meanings in addition to the surface or literal meaning. The story may have its own appeal; the images may have their own beauty, but the major emphasis is on the ulterior meanings the story and images suggest. Actually, Bunyan appears to urge this view in the rhymed preface to his own popular allegory. He builds a strong argument for figurative expressions and perceives that he has the highest authority for his using images, metaphors, or any figure of speech, and that authority is the Bible. As he asserts his confidence in the use of artistic expressions, Bunyan also readily urges readers not to dwell on the surface but 'to look within' his work, to 'turn up' the metaphors, and to 'take heed' not to misinterpret.

The reading of allegory, therefore, demands a clear focus on the literal or surface level combined with a willingness to perceive how and when various levels of meaning emerge. Careful reading also demands that readers observe that allegory refers 'upward' to the final truths of human experiences and forward to anticipated futures. This pattern seems particularly true of *The Pilgrim's Progress*.

John Bunyan fills his allegory with an array of people, with dangerous valleys and unattractive landscapes, with persecutions and humiliations, with conflicts and battles, but also with beautiful terrain, satisfying resting-places, joyous victories, and anticipation of a glorious future. No stage of the exciting journey should be overlooked. To uncover the meaning of the various stages is also the arduous task of the reader.

## 3.4 DREAM PHENOMENON

Bunyan presents his allegory within the matrix of a dream, a literary technique frequently used in the Middle Ages. Geoffrey Chaucer (*c.*1345–1400) in the *Book of the Duchess*, for example, and William Langland (*c.*1332–*c.*1400) in his *Piers Plowman* appropriate the dream as a framework for their narratives.

After he initiates the dream framework, Bunyan appears unwilling to permit the reader to forget the dream. At least sixty times in the allegory, Bunyan uses such expressions as 'now I saw in my dream' or 'then I saw in my dream'. By reminding the reader that he sees the man on a journey in a dream, the author gives a convincing realism to his illusory world. The last sentence of the allegory brings the narrator out of the dream and concludes the dream vision: 'So I awoke, and behold it was a dream'.

The dream is obviously important to Bunyan. It must not be thought of as a gateway to folly; it is a vision of reality and of revelation. The dream may show divine guidance; it may disclose a caution or warning; it may reveal a promise or a curse, and it may invite the dreamer to reform or to journey or even to write. The dream is not a lie; it is a route to truth, particularly truth that is symbolic of the human condition in relation to the greater reality of infinite or divine truth.

## 3.5 THE EMBLEM

Where Bunyan acquired his notions of emblem is difficult to resolve. Although emblems were popular in most European countries during the sixteenth and seventeenth centuries, and collections of emblems were numerous, it is doubtful that Bunyan knew many of these. He probably knew the emblematic works of the seventeenth-century writers like Francis Quarles and George Wither, but thinking in emblematic terms was a practice in practically all of his writings. Emblems were for Bunyan yet another way of writing in similitudes.

Writers of emblems hold that an object, which one can see, stimulates understanding of what one cannot literally see. In the strict sense, however, an emblem is a symbolic picture, usually accompanied by a maxim and a poem. Nevertheless, an emblematic habit of mind pervades the works of various writers, including Bunyan, although the picture is not considered to be an essential component. It is not the picture itself but rather the implicit presence of the picture that is essential.

In *The Pilgrim's Progress*, the hero confronts 'Snares, Traps . . . Nets . . . Pits, Pitfalls, deep holes' in the Valley of the Shadow of Death, simultaneously he speaks of God's candle shining on his head, of the light that guides him through darkness, and of the rising sun. An emblematist sees the candle, the light, the rising sun as known or seen objects, which point toward the presence of Christ. What is visible entails new meanings. What is seen is invested with spiritual significance.

# 4 A FEW DIRECTIONS FOR READING

In reading *The Pilgrim's Progress*, the reader ought to give primary attention, first of all, to it as a story. After reading it as an adventure story, the reader begins next to think of the work as a journey, an essential organising principle of various narratives in literature. Readers of the *Odyssey* and the *Aeneid*, for example, know that the basic structure of these works is also a journey. The journey may also take the special form of a pilgrimage, as in *The Canterbury Tales* and *The Pilgrim's Progress*, even though the pilgrimages are very different in the two works. In the Christian tradition, the pilgrimage usually depicts an individual journeying from a state of being lost to a state of blessedness. The pilgrim in *The Pilgrim's Progress* wants that blessed state in God, and the pilgrimage is the progress of a pilgrim, later named Christian, from the City of Destruction to the Celestial City.

Undeniably, John Bunyan's primary purpose is to teach and edify, but it is equally clear that both in theory and practice, he believes story to be a powerful means of releasing truth. But what a story he tells! His main character, Christian, flees from the place of destruction and starts on an adventuresome pilgrimage to the Celestial City. Along the way he encounters Pliable and Obstinate, 'wallows' in the Slough of Despond, meets theatrical Worldly Wiseman, learns in the Interpreter's House, unburdens at the Cross, 'clambers' up the Hill Difficulty, crosses the plain of Ease, fights with Apollyon, trudges through the Valley of the Shadow of Death, suffers in Doubting Castle, converses with faithful and unfaithful pilgrims, sees the ultimate goal from the Delectable Mountains, enjoys the Land of Beulah, crosses the River of Death and finally enters the Celestial City.

Bunyan unifies the narrative as a story of a pilgrimage by keeping his pilgrim always in focus as he confronts other pilgrims, a few true but many false. By numerous allusions to a goal to reach and a mission to accomplish, the author provides further awareness of a unified narrative. To add to the strength of his narrative he frequently dramatises its episodes, primarily through dialogue. He also gives full play to the senses as avenues to the mind and will. He combines sight, sound and hearing, with fear, pity, anger, horror, and other appropriate emotions to involve his readers to the point of seeming actually to experience the various situations.

*The Pilgrim's Progress* is also a dream vision, and the characteristics of the dream phenomenon receive special attention in this study. Readers should keep in mind that action in the dream world is timeless, but Bunyan includes a narrator who connects that world with the world of time.

The work is, of course, an allegory. In addition to comments made regarding allegory in the previous chapter, students might also remember that *The Pilgrim's Progress* is the type of allegory wherein every episode corresponds to a literal reality; every episode exists coherently in itself even though it has a special relation to the pilgrimage as a whole. Bunyan thought of allegory as the way words set forth one thing by another, primarily through a continuous central metaphor. Through the central metaphor of the journey, he shows the stages of a pilgrimage, filled both with struggles and triumphs, of his traveller from the City of Destruction to the Celestial City. Each stage becomes credible to the one who recognises that Bunyan views Biblical imperatives and a body of belief as informing sources of each experience. The interconnections and criss-crossings of each mortal experience are important, but what the experience suggests in terms of the spiritual is of primary significance. What the author does then is to present a structure of images; the reader sees the images as well as the precepts for the spiritual growth of the human soul. The informing source for the precepts is 'the Book' in Christian's hand, but Bunyan never suggests a separation between the metaphorical language of the Bible (the Book) and the truth it expresses.

Students will also find helpful a study of the settings of the allegory. It is not enough simply to say that settings provide the background. Such settings as the Valley of the Shadow of Death or the Plain of Ease express states of consciousness or states of the soul and show by analogy the condition of the soul as the true pilgrim travels in the

Way to the Celestial City. The streets and buildings of Vanity Fair represent, somewhat overtly, aspects of well-known fairs of contemporaneous market towns, while at the same time they suggest the worldliness which a Christian pilgrim inevitably encounters.

Some attention might be given to various levels of allegory. Simply to be aware of these levels may be challenging to a reader. To attempt to comb through each stage and each encounter to discover various levels is hardly an assignment that will lure students to Bunyan. To mention a few levels, however, might prove helpful. There is, of course, the level of the individual pilgrimage from the City of Destruction to the Celestial City.

As Bunyan suggests throughout the allegory, there is a pronounced Biblical level which follows some of the major outlines of the Old and New Testaments. Early in the allegory, for example, Bunyan links the Old Testament story of the safe journey of the Israelites with his selected metaphor of the journey. From the New Testament, Bunyan refers to the Gospel of Mark when Christian meets the Shining Ones at the Cross, to Ephesians when Christian puts on his armour, to Romans when he defeats Apollyon, and to multiple stories and images.

A theological level permeates the allegory. A reader observes this particularly in Christian's being set apart or 'elected' to make the journey, and then, after heeding the call to go on the pilgrimage, he exercises faith, repents of his wrongs, seeks forgiveness, grows in his new-found life, and perseveres to the end. The journey Christian takes is a pattern of Puritan theology.

The historical level is less pervasive than the Biblical and theological, but it too is an integral part of the allegory. To turn again to the Vanity Fair episode, the reader here observes Bunyan satirically suggesting that the secular world bases its well-being on upholding the economic systems of the world. All of these levels, however, are not equally present at the same time.

As readers proceed through *The Pilgrim's Progress*, it will enhance understanding of the work if they observe the narrator. He appears to be something like a wise author, though not always objective, in his narrative and linguistic choices. He is also a minor figure in the foreground revealing moral and religious choices. Expect no neutral position from the Dreamer–Narrator of *The Pilgrim's Progress*.

The Dreamer's primary function is to connect the world of the Christian Pilgrim on his journey with the 'real' world, or with the world of the reader. We are especially aware of his insistence on belonging to the reader's world by the repeated phrase, 'Then I saw in my Dream' and by variations such as ' . . . as I remember my Dream . . . ', and 'I saw then in my Dream . . . '. Emphatic in his desire that the reader understand his function, he says, for example, 'No man can imagine unless he has seen and heard as I did . . . '. At times he appears to sense the serious responsibility of his role. He states, for instance, 'One thing I would not let slip, I took notice that now poor Christian was so confounded that he did not know his own voice: and thus I perceived it'.

The Dreamer also talks to various characters in the dream-vision world. When Help pulls Christian out of a miry slough, the Dreamer–Narrator says, 'Then I stepped to him that plukt him out, and said; Sir, wherefore . . . is it that *this* Plat is not mended, that poor Travellers might go thither with more security?' At other times, the narrator pauses and meditates on what he sees and hears. When Christian comes to the end of the Valley of the Shadow of Death, the narrator steps before the reader and reflects: 'Now I saw in my Dream, that at the end of this Valley lay blood, bones, ashes, and mangled bodies of men, even of Pilgrims that had gone this way formerly: And while I was musing what should be the reason . . . ' (p. 54). He almost diverts attention from the story in such statements, but he shows an awareness of the cost of being a pilgrim.

On other occasions the narrator interprets the interior pain of a character or thinks himself capable of interpreting motives. When Christian goes in search of his parchment roll, which he loses while asleep, the narrator muses: 'But all the way he went back, who can sufficiently set forth the sorrow of *Christian's* heart? sometimes he sighed, sometimes he wept, and often times he chid himself . . . ' (p. 36). And when Christian leads Hopeful into a meadow that ultimately leads them to doubt and despair, Hopeful explains why he went along: '*I was afraid on't at first, and therefore gave you that gentle caution. I would have spoke plainer, but that you are older than I*' (p. 92).

Statements which indicate the narrator's supreme knowledge of people, motives and places are on many pages of the allegory. When Christian and Hopeful enter the land of Beulah, they 'had more rejoicing' than in parts 'more remote from the Kingdom'. Here the sun shines night and day, and the pilgrims find 'abundance' of what they 'had sought for in all their Pilgrimage'.

The Dreamer–Narrator is also so perceptive and knowledgeable that he is able to caution others about the Way one must go to the final end. He rejoices when Christian and Hopeful enter the new city and reports somewhat poignantly, 'And after that, they shut up the Gates: which when I had seen, I wished myself among them' (p. 132). But he can also sound an indirect word of warning. Ignorance comes to the Gates without a certificate for entrance and immediately comes to destruction. The narrator observes: 'Then I saw that there was a way to Hell, even from the Gates of Heaven' (p. 133).

To understand what the narrator does is important, and to help us see his role is the purpose of this rather lengthy discussion. Students may believe that he distracts from the story, but on occasions he assists readers in looking and listening more clearly to the dream-vision.

In reading and studying *The Pilgrim's Progress*, students will do well to keep in mind the words of the distinguished scholar James Thorpe on John Bunyan: 'He brought the language of prose narrative into contact with the human world, and he thought fit to have his characters use the speech of real men and women. He developed dialogue which could present the inner world of the mind and feeling as well as the outer world of language and action.' Thorpe also added: ' . . . he was bold enough to take as his subject a central theme in the Christian tradition, the salvation of man, and to deal with his subject in literary form . . . '. It will indeed be satisfying if readers of this book find directions in their reading of *The Pilgrim's Progress* that will lead them somewhere near the above tribute.

# 5 SUMMARY AND COMMENTARY

## 5.1 BUNYAN'S ATTITUDE TOWARDS THE METAPHORICAL JOURNEY

Writers on *The Pilgrim's Progress* usually begin with the actual story. Before the story begins, Bunyan apparently feels that he should write a defence of the form his work takes. In lines closer to doggerel than to poetry, he pinpoints characteristics of literary art, especially in his insistence upon the transforming power of the imagination. These lines constitute the rhymed preface to his allegory. He obviously feels compelled to justify his allegorical mode, perhaps to those critics, real or imagined, who would expect only literal, expository statements from one who holds his religious convictions. To explain that literary art is no enemy of truth, he summons the authority of the Bible and insists:

> *The Prophets used much by Metaphors*
> *To set forth Truth; Yea, who so considers*
> *Christ, his Apostles too, shall plainly see,*
> *That Truths to this day in such Mantles be.* (p. 4)

What Bunyan suggests, first of all, is that the Bible is an artistic book, and metaphors frequently embody its truth. He therefore has the highest authority for writing metaphorically. At the same time, there is no stronger way to teach or to show truth than through metaphors.

In the Bible Bunyan sees that familiar and commonplace words like seeds, camels, a lost sheep, a lost coin, and numerous ordinary terms may become suggestive of a truth or reality beyond themselves.

Convinced that metaphorical language tells us something about ourselves as well as about Someone beyond ourselves, and that a reader sees the 'something' or 'Someone' through metaphor, Bunyan argues that 'base things usher in Divine'. To show resemblances, to depict connections, to express more than the familiar, and to unite the ordinary and literal with the mysterious and transcendent are the ways of metaphor. For Bunyan, a writer's work is not less true if written in metaphorical language.

While recognizing all this Bunyan also suggests that what he attempts to do has a relationship to what God became in the Incarnation. That relationship may be briefly explained in this way: as the Incarnate God, the Word, is the physical embodiment of the Divine and transcendent, so the written word is capable of capturing and merging the profoundly transcendent in the physical and immediate. As a writer, Bunyan believes that he must incarnate the spiritual in terms of the literal. For support of this view, he says, 'Truth in Swadling–clouts' (an obvious reference to the baby in swaddling clothes)

> *Informs the Judgement, rectifies the Mind,*
> *Pleases the Understanding, makes the Will*
> *Submit; the Memory too it doth fill*
> *With what doth our Imagination please;*
> *Likewise, it tends our troubles to appease.* (p. 5)

In only a few lines, Bunyan clearly demonstrates his belief in metaphorical language or his belief in the power of allegory. To a great extent he also depicts his arduous task as a writer of allegory: to find a language that will image forth a perception of reality in a manner that not only embodies truth but also penetrates the judgement, the mind, the understanding, the will; indeed, the entirety of the human being.

To the readers or critics who argue that they want truth, not 'feigned words', Bunyan assures them that 'feigned words' can make 'truth to spangle'. He literally pleads with readers to understand that metaphorical language and truth need not be incompatible. He also finds pleasure in writing the allegory, but he also thinks of himself as a steward of a vision, and he must also interpret the vision. He probes beneath the surface, unearths what uncritical minds and unhoned imagination may never see, and invests what he sees with earnest meaning. The very fact that Bunyan reasons so clearly in attempting to justify his form and method reveals the depth of his commitment to 'similitude' as a way of depicting God's truth.

## 5.2  THE JOURNEY FROM THE CITY OF DESTRUCTION TO THE CELESTIAL CITY

Through the central literary figure of a journey, Bunyan shows in *The Pilgrim's Progress* the stages of a Christian pilgrimage from the City of Destruction to the Celestial City. The chief character, Pilgrim (later called Christian) flees from his family and neighbours and begins a journey which takes him into numerous conflicts in the world, and yet he goes beyond and ultimately out of the world.

As has already been pointed out, Bunyan sets the journey of his pilgrim within the matrix of a dream. The narrator walks through 'the wilderness of this world', arrives at a 'certain place' and 'dreams a dream'. Bunyan immediately lifts his dream to the metaphorical level as he writes of the world as a wilderness through which his pilgrim travels on his way to the Celestial City.

Pilgrim's travels will take him to the Wicket-Gate and to the Cross. His experiences include growth and understanding in places such as the Interpreter's House and the House Beautiful and in conversations with shepherds in the Delectable Mountains, and with people like Evangelist, Faithful, and Hopeful. The journey also entails severe conflicts in the Valley of Humiliation and the Valley of the Shadow of Death, persecution in Vanity Fair, suffering in Doubting Castle, encounters with Ignorance, By-ends, and Little-faith, and the allurement of By-Path Meadow and the Enchanted Ground. At a place called Beulah, the gate of the Celestial City is in sight. Before Pilgrim can enter the new city, he has one more severe task, the River of Death, which provides 'no bridge to go over'. Once through this river, Christian enters the glorious new city, beholding sights far more beautiful than he had ever imagined.

Bunyan tells us that his purpose in writing is to 'chalk out' the journey of one who seeks 'the everlasting prize'. Yet what is the meaning of all the stages suggested by the numerous capital-lettered words? And how are the various stages related to the journey in its entirety? To find an answer to these questions the whole book must be explored.

## 5.3 TO THE CROSS

The work begins with the narrator stating that, as he 'walk'd through the wilderness of this world', he 'lighted on a certain place', and lay down to sleep. As he slept, he 'dreamed a dream'. In that dream, he saw a man 'clothed with raggs standing in a certain place, with his face from his own House, a Book in his hand, and a great burden upon his Back'. When he read from the book, he 'wept and trembled' and cried 'what shall I do?' The answers to problems posed by this cry constitute the major features of the dream.

Christian tells Evangelist of his plight and receives from him a Parchment-roll and strong counsel to go directly to the Wicket-gate. Christian follows this advice and begins to run toward the gate. When his family perceive that he is leaving them, they begin to cry after him to return, but Christian places his fingers in his ears and continues to run and to cry out, 'Life, Life, Eternal Life'.

Neighbours also join in the family's plea for his return. Some mock him; others threaten him. One of his neighbours, Obstinate, thinks Christian is a fool or a 'brain-sick fellow'; another neighbour, Pliable, who joins Christian, enjoys hearing from him about 'an endless kingdom' and 'Crowns of Glory', 'Seraphims' and 'Cherubins'. In fact he wants Christian to run faster so that they will soon realise the promise of these splendours which await them. To run faster is difficult for Christian, for he still has a burden on his back. Pliable has only surface interest, however, in making the journey with Christian, for when the two journeyers reach the 'Slew of Dispond' he loses interest in any further statements about future joys. He struggles out of the slough and returns to the City of Destruction.

Christian, with the aid of Help, who shows him the steps which lead out of the mire, escapes the slough and continues alone on the journey. After a short distance he encounters Mr Worldly-Wiseman from the town of Carnal Policy. He advises Christian to ignore the counsel of Evangelist and to turn toward Mr Legality's house for assistance. As he heads there, his burden grows heavier and he becomes dreadfully afraid. About this time, he sees Evangelist coming to meet him. Evangelist rebukes him for not following doctrines, listens to Christian's description of the person he had just left and immediately recognises him as Mr Worldly-Wiseman. He further counsels Christian, forgives him for his lack of prudence, and sends him on his way. In a spirit of humility and repentance,

Christian goes to the Wicket-gate. Good Will opens the gate and tells him of the way he *must* go if he is to complete the journey to the Celestial City.

Christian now goes to the Interpreter's House where he sees a large number of emblematic pictures. Some of the pictures are biblical; others are not, but all are supported by scriptural texts. The first picture is that of a 'very grave' person (probably Evangelist) with eyes lifted towards heaven, the 'best of Books' in his hand and the 'law of truth' on his lips. The Interpreter tells Christian that this person is to be his guide. The next picture is that of a 'large Parlour' full of dust. When a man begins to sweep, the dust flies about in such abundance that Christian almost chokes before a girl pours water on it and so cleanses the air. The Interpreter explains to Christian that the parlour is man's heart; the dust is original sin; the one who sweeps is the Law, and the girl who sprinkles the water is the Gospel; just as she cleanses the air with the water so also is the soul made clean by faith in the Gospel.

Christian next sees Passion and Patience in a little room. Passion is without contentment, and Patience is very quiet. The Interpreter explains that Passion is given a bag of 'Treasure' but wastes it immediately, while Patience is willing to wait quietly for any possessions. Passion typifies those who grasp for earthly possessions, but Patience represents those who look forward to heavenly possessions, which last forever.

Next Christian sees a picture of the Devil pouring water on a fire while Christ stands behind a wall feeding the fire with oil. The fire is symbolic of Christ's grace in the heart; the whole scene suggests that Christian is able to overcome the work of the Devil only through Christ's grace.

Then the Interpreter leads Christian to a palace, in front of which sits a man at a table, writing down names of those permitted to enter. A man with a sword fights his way into the palace. After viewing the scene, Christian, with a smile on his face, tells the Interpreter that he thinks he 'knows the meaning of this'.

The Interpreter leads Christian into a dark room and shows him a man in a cage. Following a long discussion, the man discloses to Christian that he is beyond all hope, is unable to repent, and is in an iron cage of despair. He accepts responsibility for his sad plight, for he says he has despised Christ and His righteousness.

The final scene is that of a man who describes his dream of the fearful day of judgement. The Interpreter admonishes Christian to keep in his memory all that he has seen. After viewing the pictures and listening to interpretations of them, he continues the journey by a wall that is called Salvation until he comes to the Cross. At the Cross the heavy burden falls from his back and falls into a sepulchre below. Three Shining Ones appear and tell him his sins are now forgiven. They give him new clothes, put a mark on his forehead, and present him with a Roll with a seal upon it, which he is to show and 'give in' at the Celestial Gate.

## Commentary

Christian, the central character, has read in the book in his hand and discovered that he is a sinner. He wants to be relieved of the burden of his sin. Evangelist (one who preaches the Bible), directs him to the Wicket-Gate or to Christ. He flees his family, hears the mocking of neighbours, and friends, but blocks the calls of the world by placing his fingers in his ears. He continues his journey only to fall into a miry slough which reveals the onslaught of despair, but Help shows him 'the steps' to overcome despair. These steps are promises or texts of Scripture which show God's mercy.

Worldy-Wiseman typifies the wisdom of this world which scorns the cross, and Legality is the tenor of the Law untouched by Grace. The Wicket-gate is Christ, on whose mercy Christian must throw himself. The Interpreter's House shows some of the basic truths which are essential in strengthening Christian's spiritual life. The Cross is the sacrifice of Christ's blood, the only route whereby Christian may lose his burden and his sins be forgiven him. The Roll is the merciful pardon of Christ, through which Christian is a new man.

The entire allegory turns on the sacrifice of Christ on the cross. The burden of sin falling from Christian's shoulders signifies that Christ's sacrificial death is the only means of salvation from sin. The mark which the angel places on his forehead clearly indicates that Christian is now marked by God to continue his Christian pilgrimage.

## 5.4 FROM THE CROSS THROUGH THE VALLEY OF THE SHADOW OF DEATH

Following the experiences at the Cross, Christian now begins the joy and pain of his conversion. He next passes three men fast asleep, with fetters on their heels. Their names are Simple, Sloth, and Presumption. The indifference of these men troubles Christian. Equally troubling is the attitude of the next two 'pilgrims' whom he meets, Formalist and Hypocrisy. To make the long arduous journey which Christian undertakes is not the desire of these two men. They attempt to take a short cut. At the Hill Difficulty, where Christian painfully climbs upward on his hands and knees, Formalist and Hypocrisy seek roads which go around the hill, but these roads lead to destruction. After struggling almost to the top of the hill, Christian lies down to rest. He pulls his Roll out of his clothing, reads from it, and looks again at the new garment which he received at the Cross. Relaxed and refreshed, Christian falls asleep in the pleasant arbour. While asleep, he loses his Roll.

After refreshing himself, Christian continues to the top of the Hill Difficulty where Mistrust and Timorous meet him, going in the opposite direction. They talk of lions in the way, and Christian becomes afraid, but only for a moment. He resolutely tells these two travellers that he *must venture*. As he feels in his bosom for his Roll in order that he might read from it, Christian discovers that he has lost it. He soon realises that he left it at the pleasant arbour where he had slept. Returning to that spot, he recovers his Roll and goes on his way. He soon sees the lions, but also discovers that they are chained and that they guard the entrance to the House Beautiful, where the porter receives him.

The House Beautiful is another place for instruction, conversation and relaxation. In the House Beautiful he meets Discretion, Piety, Charity and Prudence. Here he also receives a new armour for his journey: sword, shield, helmet, breastplate, All-Prayer, and shoes that 'would not wear out'. Thus equipped, Christian leaves the House Beautiful and descends to the Valley of Humiliation, one of the most horrible places of the entire journey. Here he meets the foul fiend, Apollyon, who attempts to dissuade Christian from following God and to declare his allegiance to Satan. The challenge from Apollyon leads to a fierce battle. The combat lasts for more than 'half a day', and is by no means one-sided. When it appears that Apollyon lacks only one blow to finish Christian, he receives such a 'deadly thrust' from his opponent that he spreads his dragon wings and departs. No more does Apollyon confront Christian, but his disappearance by no means marks the end of Christian's battles.

Following the victory over Apollyon, Christian gives thanks for his triumph, heals his wounds with leaves of the tree of Life, refreshes himself with bread and wine, and addresses himself to the next stage of the journey. This is the Valley of the Shadow of Death, and men who were 'almost in the valley' describe to Christian, in shocked tones, something of its horrors. They declare that the valley is 'as dark as pitch', and in this dark place are 'Hobgoblins, Satyrs, and Dragons of the Pit'. The men also hear sounds of terror: 'a continual howling and yelling, as of a People under unutterable misery', and they see the dreadful sight of death with wings spread over the valley. After listening to these reports, Christian insists that 'this is my way to the desired Haven'. As they turn away, Christian plunges ahead from hazard to hazard through the Valley of the Shadow of Death.

Among the dangers are snares, traps, gins, nets and pitfalls. There are devils who whisper blasphemies into his ears, and there is the constant feeling that someone pursues or haunts him. Perhaps the worst of all horrors is the sensation of being utterly alone. In a moment of deepest despair, he thinks he hears the voice of a man going before him and saying, 'Though I walk through the valley of the shadow of death, I will fear no evil for thou art with me.' The voice is the voice of Faithful, another true pilgrim, whom Christian meets in the light of the following day after he emerges from the valley. In the glory of the new sunrise, Christian emerges from the Valley of the Shadow of Death.

### Commentary

Christian is in the way he *must* go if he is to enter the Celestial City. He meets those who have no sense of urgency regarding their spiritual plight. He also meets those who seek not the Christian route or who think they can be in the way even though they avoid the Cross. Formalist and Hypocrisy do not come in at the Wicket-Gate or by the blood of Christ. They experience no conversion but rely on forms of worship. At the Hill Difficulty, the picture of spiritual struggle, they refuse to pay the price. While finding routes that cut around struggles and difficulties, both come separately to grief. Christian also learns that his Christian journey only begins, rather than ends, at the Cross. His falling asleep in the arbour and losing his Roll indicates that he should not presume that the Christian life is one of sloth and ease.

House Beautiful suggests fellowship with believing Christians and growth in understanding of the faith. Here Christian learns to cultivate moral and spiritual virtues. Here, too, he receives prepara-

---

tion for the battles ahead. These battles are facets of the various spiritual combats of the true pilgrim. One of the strongest spiritual terrors which Christian endures is the conflict with the power of evil as seen in the battle with Apollyon. The battle is not exclusively physical; it is also psychological.

The Valley of the Shadow of Death shows the horrible temptations that the Christian pilgrim encounters; it also suggests the terrible aloneness which a pilgrim may endure. In the midst of such ghastly experiences, the Christian pilgrim also overcomes the enemy and finds deliverance by demonstrating spiritual weapons: the shield of faith and the sword of the Spirit. In his triumph, Christian knows a new virtue, faith, symbolised by his new travelling companion, Faithful.

## 5.5 FROM THE VALLEY OF THE SHADOW OF DEATH THROUGH VANITY FAIR

Following the meeting of Christian with Faithful, the two pilgrims compare notes of their travels as they continue the journey. Faithful tells Christian of his adventures which are surely less exciting than the experiences of Christian. A woman named Wanton had tempted Faithful to turn away from his journey, but when he refused, she had railed at him. Later, he met an 'old man', Adam the First, who implored Faithful to serve him, but when he refused, the old man scorned him. As he ascended the Hill Difficulty, a man overtook him and knocked him down. Christian identified the man as Moses. Faithful continued the account of his 'trials' by relating his meeting, in the Valley of Humiliation, with Discontent, who had tried to dissuade him from continuing the journey. He also met Shame, who had ridiculed his Christian life. As the two pilgrims continue to discuss their experiences, Faithful looks 'on one side' and sees a man named Talkative. This glib man is able to use with precision the language of the two Christian pilgrims. Whether one wishes to talk of 'things heavenly or things earthly', Talkative is perfectly capable of engaging in lengthy conversation. He almost deceives Faithful into believing that he too is a pilgrim eager to arrive at the Celestial City. Christian, however, also knows Talkative and gives a prolonged discussion on the true nature of this loquacious man. It is Faithful who pointedly characterises Talkative in the terse statement, 'Well, I see that Saying and Doing are two different things'. True to his nature, Talkative continues to talk and talk until he unconsciously reveals his own hypocrisy, and he shows himself in his own shallow life covered over with words without substance.

After Talkative's departure from the two pilgrims, Evangelist visits them again, praises them for their progress in their pilgrimage, and warns them to be prepared for the death of one or both of them in the town of Vanity. The pilgrims enter the crowded market of Vanity Fair with its 'Britain Row, French Row, Italian Row, where several sorts of Vanities are to be sold'. Vanity Fair had been set up almost five thousand years before by the devils Beelzebub, Apollyon, Legion and their colleagues to tempt all pilgrims on the journey to the Celestial City. Also inherent in the episode is the Biblical text, 'vanity of vanities, all is vanity' (Ecclesiastes 1:2). Christian and Faithful draw attention to themselves by their clothing, their speech, and their lack of interest in the merchandise for sale. Their response to a question concerning what they wish to buy is simply, 'We buy the Truth'. For their singleness of purpose, uncompromising views and strange appearance, they are put in prison, exposed in a cage, and finally brought to trial.

The presiding judge is Lord Hategood, and the jurors in the packed jury include such characters as Mr Blind-man, Mr No-good, Mr Malice, Mr Love-lust, Mr Enmity and Mr Implacable. The pilgrims are charged with disturbing the peace. Envy, Superstition, and Pickthank condemn Faithful to death and advise that he be 'put to the most cruel death that could be invented'. No form of cruelty is lacking: they scourge him, buffet him, lance his flesh with knives, stone him, prick him with swords and burn him to ashes. Following this horrible death, a chariot drawn by horses takes Faithful up through the clouds to the Celestial City. Christian 'was remanded back to prison'. After 'a space' of time, Christian miraculously escapes and a new friend, Hopeful, joins him on the pilgrimage. Observing the sufferings of Faithful, Hopeful chooses to become a pilgrim.

**Commentary**

For his description of the Valley of the Shadow of Death, Bunyan may well be drawing on his own recollections of horrible temptations in his own life (he vividly depicts these times of terror in his autobiography, *Grace Abounding*). At the moments of intense despair and extreme doubt, the only means of deliverance is strong faith in God's promises.

The account of Faithful and Christian is simply an exchange of shared experiences as believers. Both pilgrims are in the way they must go, but some experiences vary slightly. Faithful's reference, for example, to the Old Man who gives him 'a deadly twitch back' when he tries to escape from his cajolement suggests the power of original sin, the sin inherited from Adam.

The episode with Talkative, the glib 'pilgrim' who knew how to talk religion but not how to practise it, shows he is a hypocrite, and the hypocrites of the world are completely unaware of the costly price of making the arduous journey from the City of Destruction to the Celestial City. They can talk, but they refuse to *be* or to *do*.

Bunyan probably used the fairs held in the market towns of his own era as a model for Vanity Fair. It is also possible that he modelled Lord Hategood (the judge) on the magistrate who had presided at his own trial. Vanity Fair provides a vivid description of this world from which Christian must separate himself: he must separate himself from its priorities and its values, but he is profoundly *in* the world and must exemplify Christian virtues in it. Whatever the persecutions, the Christian must remain faithful (as both Christian and Faithful do) even though one may die for his beliefs. Few episodes show the plight of the Christian in his contemporary world as clearly as does Vanity Fair. Bunyan's own experiences obviously flood the trial scene as he recalls his ordeal before a jury after his own arrest.

## 5.6  FROM VANITY FAIR TO THE DELECTABLE MOUNTAINS

Following the intense dramatic action of Vanity Fair, there now occurs a rather quiet period of conversation between the pilgrims, Hopeful and Christian. They meet By-ends who comes from the town of Fair-speech where By-ends has many kindred. Among these are Lord Turn-about, Lord Time-server, Mr Facing-bothways, Mr Anything, and the parson of the parish, Mr Two-tongues. By-ends admits that his family is different from those of the 'stricter sort', particularly in two ways. They never strive against 'Wind and Tide', and they are most zealous 'when religion goes in his Silver Slippers'. Although he tells Christian and Hopeful that they would find him to be a 'fair Company-keeper', By-ends loses all interest in joining them when the two pilgrims explain the conditions through which one enters into the Christian way.

Passing now across a 'delicate' plain called Ease, where at 'the further side of that Plain, was a little Hill called Lucre, and in that Hill a Silver-Mine', Christian and Hopeful see Demas who guards the mine. Demas stands 'a little off the Road, over against the Silver-Mine'. Christian and Hopeful refuse the call of Demas to stop at the mine, but By-ends and his companions (once again they come within sight) go over to Demas at his 'first beck'. The next sight for the two pilgrims is an old monument in the form of a woman transformed into the shape of a pillar. The monument is in memory of Lot's wife of the Old Testament who was turned into a pillar of salt.

As they go on their way the pilgrims enjoy an enormously beautiful landscape. There is a lovely river from which they drink, and on the banks of the river are green trees that bear all manner of fruit. On either side of the river is a pleasant meadow, beautiful with lilies, and here Christian and Hopeful lie down for rest and sleep. When they awake, they again eat of the fruit of the trees, and drink of the water of life. They enjoy these pleasures for several days and nights. When they finally leave they find the road from the river to be rough and, seeking an easier route, they stray into By-Path meadow, only to discover that this path turns out to be a departure from the way they *must* go.

Struggling to leave By-Path meadow they stop in their weariness for rest and fall asleep, only to discover later that they are close to Doubting Castle which is owned by Giant Despair. Upon discovering the pilgrims on his property, the Giant puts them in a dark dungeon in his castle. Here they remain from Wednesday to Saturday without food and water. On the first night, Giant Despair's wife, Diffidence, urges him to beat the two intruders the next morning.

The Giant complies and beats the pilgrims with a crab-tree cudgel (club). Still full of advice, Diffidence the next night urges the Giant to persuade Christian and Hopeful to take their own lives. On the following morning, Giant Despair presents the possibilities of suicide. Christian all but completely gives way to his own despair and thinks twice of taking his life, but Hopeful persuades him not to think of such action and reminds him of his numerous triumphs in past stages of his pilgrimage. Following his wife's suggestion once again, on Saturday morning Giant Despair takes Christian and Hopeful into the Castle-yard and shows them the 'bones and skulls' of previous pilgrims whom he had killed. The strength of these two pilgrims does, however, puzzle Giant Despair, for he is unable to destroy them either by 'blows' or 'counsel'. The sight of others torn to pieces adds to the feeling of despair for the pilgrims, especially Christian.

Finally, in the middle of the night, the two pilgrims begin to pray, and they pray until 'almost break of day'. Shortly before the break of the new day, Christian remembers that he has a key in his bosom called Promise which is capable of unlocking the gate to the castle. Escape is now certain; Christian turns the key in the dungeon door, and the door opens with ease. The next door, the one that leads to the Castle-yard, gives him no trouble, but the iron outer gate 'lock went damnable hard'. Giant Despair hears the noise from the gates opening, but he falls into a fit and is unable to prevent the pilgrims from leaving. When they depart, they decide to erect a pillar on which they engrave words that warn other pilgrims to avoid the route of Doubting Castle.

The dangers of Doubting Castle – and indeed most dangers of the entire journey – are past. Christian and Hopeful now come to the Delectable Mountains of Immanuel's Land, and these mountains are within sight of the Celestial City. In this idyllic land the pilgrims lean on their staves and talk to shepherds. These shepherds, Knowledge, Experience, Watchful and Sincere, take them by the hand, and lead them into their tents for food and rest. The next morning they walk on the mountains; the shepherds point out the hills of Error and of Caution, where men blinded by Giant Despair are seen walking among tombs. They are also shown a door in a hill – the byway to hell. From the hill, Clear, they attempt to look through the shepherd's perspective glass, but their hands shake so much that they cannot actually see the Celestial City, although they think they see 'something of the Glory of the place', the glory of the city towards which they journey. They are sent on their way with warnings against the flatterer, and against sleeping on the Enchanted Ground.

**Commentary**

Mr By-ends, Demas, and the memory of Lot's wife suggest the temptations of covetousness. The form of covetousness is primarily the sordid thirst for wealth. It should be noted, however, that By-ends comes into the allegory while Christian and Hopeful are discussing the uncompromising Faithful. Unlike Faithful, he lives near enough to Vanity Fair to feel at home, yet sufficiently removed from it to disclaim any relation to it when in the company of pilgrims. He is the kind of character who would care little for the church or religion if it were not for many side advantages, including money, popularity and respectability.

Peace and conflict alternate in this section and a pleasant place called Ease is part of the pilgrims' experiences, but even Ease is never free from peril. Ease has in it the hill of Lucre with the silver mine. The hill is a 'little' hill; this is one of those apparently small but insidious temptations that lure pilgrims. The silver mine is not only a blot on the physical landscape but also on the moral land-scape – avarice is so concentrated that it becomes a dominant passion. Demas stands in a gentlemanly manner and calls to travellers to 'come and see'. The temptation of seeing perhaps suggests one of the most subtle temptations, the lust of the eyes. It is to Christian's credit that he does not swerve from the right path. The temptations in this section, however, are not those of clear and absolute right and wrong, but Christian refuses to become engulfed by the potentially dangerous. Unlike By-ends, he is uncompromising in his behaviour.

In Doubting Castle Christian's resoluteness is not as convincing as it is on the plain of Ease. The whole episode shows that Christian can lose his way even far along in the journey. Tormenting doubts and agonising fears all but overwhelm him. It is only when he remembers the promises of the Book, from which he read at the very beginning of the journey, that he finds hope and release. In this new state of hope, both pilgrims experience a lofty spiritual vision, especially as they stand on Mount Clear with the shepherds, who offer the pilgrims an opportunity to see the new city. It is true, however, that they still see blurringly. The four shepherds suggest characteristics of the mature Christian, perhaps of the Christian leader. Knowledge is the first – a mature Christian must possess knowledge, especially of the Scriptures. Experience comes next, reminding pilgrims of all eras that knowledge must be intertwined with life. Then comes Watchful, counselling caution at all times. Last is Sincere, a word that prac-tically identifies personal character. No amount of knowledge or experience or caution can mean a great deal if the pilgrim lacks sincerity. Once again Bunyan wishes to emphasise the qualities of a true pilgrim.

## 5.7 FROM THE DELECTABLE MOUNTAINS TO THE CELESTIAL CITY

The adventures immediately following the episodes of Doubting Castle and the Delectable Mountains are, as adventures, subdued. The pilgrims have a lengthy, but introductory, conversation with 'a brisk lad', Ignorance, who seeks to enter upon the journey from the town of Conceit. Christian maintains that this would-be pilgrim must enter by the Wicket-Gate, but Ignorance sees no reason why his good living by right rules is not sufficient qualification for his entrance onto the journey. They meet Little-Faith with whom Christian deals gently, but not without recognising his meagre spirituality. They encounter Flatterer who utters not one single word of praise and leads the pilgrims astray. Flatterer throws a net over them and they remain entangled until a shining One frees them.

There is a meeting with Atheist who laughs at them for undertaking such a tedious journey, a manifest way of showing ignorance. Sleep almost overcomes them in the Enchanted Ground, until Hopeful gives a lengthy discourse on his spiritual experiences. Although the conversation, particularly Christian's incisive analysis of their experiences, is a somewhat severe mental exercise for a drowsy region it succeeds in keeping the pilgrims awake and moving towards the journey's end. When Ignorance joins them again the conversation turns to justification through Christ, but Ignorance dislikes the subject and drops back.

They now come to the beautiful land of Beulah where the sun shines night and day, where the birds sing continually, and where 'every day the flowers appear in the earth'. They are now out of reach of Apollyon and Giant Despair, yet just ahead is the River of Death. They question the possibility of another route to the Celestial City, but there is emphatically no way to escape the River. As they enter the water, Christian begins to sink and to become dreadfully afraid, but Hopeful constantly encourages him until they reach the other side of the River. After the crossing, angels come out to meet them and lead the pilgrims to the gate of the gloriously beautiful city. We lose sight of Christian and Hopeful in a blaze of light amid the strains of celestial music and the glorious sound of ringing bells. After this beautiful scene, there is a final paragraph. Ignorance confidently comes up to the gate and faces the grim reality of his lacking the essential certificate to gain entrance into the Celestial City.

# Commentary

The early encounters in this last section suggest temptations that are common to man, particularly to those who are more mature in the faith. The struggle for the pilgrims is not as violent as some of their earlier experiences, but the temptations are equally dangerous and perhaps more subtle. In the midst of these temptations, the conversation between the two pilgrims concentrates on the righteousness of Christ, on grace, on justification by faith, and on various matters associated with the route to the Celestial City.

Bunyan does more through these conversations than simply give to his pilgrims an opportunity to pass away the hours. He is emphasising the need for and the efficacy of shared experiences among fellow believers. By the same token, Ignorance is unable to share Christian experiences with the pilgrims, for he believes that man is able by himself to earn salvation, thus implying that Christ's sacrifice at the Cross was unnecessary. Readers know that the Cross is the starting-point for the Christian experience, but Ignorance bypasses the Cross, and he is also ignorant of the mutual benefits of shared experiences.

One of Bunyan's most poetical conceptions is the land of Beulah. The language used to describe Beulah recalls the beautiful poetry of Canticles, Isaiah and the Revelation. This land is a paradise which probably suggests the lofty spiritual vision of the two pilgrims nearing their journey's end, a vision no longer a matter of glimpses gained through a glass. This spiritual vision is now an habitual condition of the soul. Beulah also represents a stage of unusually close communion with God, possible to him who knows the struggles as well as the joys of the Christian way. But death still awaits these pilgrims. The River of Death – or death itself – is not glossed over; it is a reality that must be faced. The journey for the Christian is a struggle to the very end. When the journey is over, however, the pilgrim who has the 'Certificate' to present at the gate of the new city enters into a life of unparalleled glory. But the one who deliberately ignores the Certificate and is impervious to the route the pilgrims take has no part with them in their great pageant of glory.

## THE SECOND PART OF *THE PILGRIM'S PROGRESS*

A few observations should now be made on the second part of *The Pilgrim's Progress*, published in 1684. Although the engaging story of

Christian's struggles and travels in Part One somewhat overshadow the less intense experiences of the travelling group in Part Two, the latter is not a mere repetitious tracing of the stages of Christian's pilgrimage. Landmarks are similar in both journeys, but reactions differ. To grasp the character of the second part one must remember that the focus is on a *group* and the route they take as they follow the instructive markers left by Christian. In Part One, the focus is not on a group but on one individual and on the way he *must* go.

There are, in fact, many interconnections between the two parts, but the variations occur frequently enough to make the sequel an appealing story in itself. To read the two parts in close sequence assists a reader in observing how Christian prepares the way for Christiana and her entourage. The recurring mention of the family left behind in the City of Destruction, however, certainly provokes a reader to wonder what ever happened to the wife and children. In the opening section of Part Two, Bunyan suggests that he has not quite completed his story; he refers to Christian's departure from his family but says that his busy life has kept him from his desired travels to the city from which Christian set out. At present, however, he takes up his lodging 'about a mile off the place' of the beginnings of Christian's journey, sleeps, and dreams again.

It is not our intention to study Part Two of *The Pilgrim's Progress* with the same analysis as in the treatment of Part One. Some attention to landmarks of the journey, and similarities and differences between Christian's pilgrimage and that of Christiana and her entourage must be observed. The various literary techniques also command attention.

## 1  To the Cross

As the narrator sleeps and dreams, an aged gentleman, a new figure in Part Two called Sagacity, comes by, and discussion begins regarding Christian who had left the City of Destruction. Christian is now no longer a struggling pilgrim but, according to Sagacity, he is so much in the affections of the 'Prince' of another country that the Prince looks upon the indignities 'cast upon Christian' as if they were done unto himself. The old man promises to tell the narrator about Christian's wife, called Christiana, because she has now become a pilgrim, and about their four boys, all of whom are now in 'the way' Christian took.

Christiana recalls her behaviour towards her husband, admits her wrong and regrets her thinking of his desperate cry for deliverance from his burden as no more than a state of melancholy. As she sleeps she also dreams, and her dream-within-the-dream consists of three scenes: she sees a 'broad Parchment' on which there is a record of her sins and she cries aloud for mercy; she next sees 'two very ill favoured ones' who fear they may lose her as they had lost her husband. Finally, she sees Christian in 'a place of bliss', enjoying the heavenly music and understanding the conversation of the immortals.

The morning following the dream, Secret, a heavenly messenger, comes to bring a letter from Christian's King; the contents state that *'the King would have her do as did Christian'*. Secret further advises that she go to the *Wicket Gate*. To linger is no option in Christiana's mind; she calls to her children and requests that they pack, for they are on their way to 'the Gate' that leads to the Celestial Country. Almost as soon as Christiana makes the decision, two visitors, Mrs Timorous, daughter of the man whom Christian met on the Hill Difficulty, and Mercy, come with opposing views. Mrs Timorous attempts to stop Christiana going on such a dangerous journey, supporting her tirade by referring to the 'wise men', Obstinate and Pliable, who refused to continue the journey with Christian. Mercy, however, yearns to go with Christiana and laments for the state of those left behind. In the company of Mercy, Christiana and her four sons begin the pilgrimage to the Wicket Gate.

The Slough of Despond all but brings the travellers to a complete stop, but Mercy, urging boldness but caution, gets the little group moving over the slough. Just before the travellers arrive at the Wicket Gate, Sagacity leaves the narrator to 'dream out' his dream by himself. He thinks he sees the group go up to the Gate where Christiana knocks, only to be greeted at first by a barking dog. Ultimately the Keeper answers, takes her by the hand, leads her inside, and requests that the little children come in with her; but then he shuts the gate. A trumpeter comes and entertains the travellers, but Mercy is not among them; she is outside the gate, trembling and crying from fear. Christiana intercedes for Mercy, who continues to knock, but when the Keeper opens the gate he discovers her in a swoon. After he brings her inside and requests someone to revive her, he leads them up 'To the top of the Gate' and shows them how they are saved from sins. It is wise to remember, however, that the Wicket Gate is, as in Christian's case, the point of crisis – a place of choice and the way a believer must go.

As the pilgrims continue their journey, they go down the side of a wall that separates them from the Devil's garden. Christiana's sons eat of the fruit that hangs over this wall towards the travellers. Shortly, two 'ill-favored' strangers approach and 'lay hands' on the women, but one called Reliever arrives in time to save them from the ruffians. However, he rebukes them for not requesting a guide or a 'conductor'.

The next stage on the journey is the House of the Interpreter. To the surprise of no reader, the pilgrims visit a number of rooms and see many of the same emblems and pictures which Christian had studied previously. They see the man in the iron cage, the man and his dream of judgement, the man who cut his way through his enemies, and the picture 'of the biggest of them all', the portrait of a minister. Then they see the man with a muckrake in his hand, an ugly spider on the wall of a spacious room, a hen and her chickens, a slaughterhouse where a butcher kills sheep, a garden with a great variety of flowers, a field of straw, a robin with a 'great spider in his mouth', and a tree rotten on the inside. Following the tour of the rooms, the Interpreter sits with his guests at a bountiful meal, with music provided by minstrels. When the song and music end, Christiana and Mercy tell their stories of the beginnings of their pilgrimage. The Interpreter converses more with the two women than he did with Christian and he fills his speech with scriptural quotations, not always particularly pertinent to the occasion. With the women his manner is almost excessively tender, as he calls them 'sweetheart' or 'my darling'. After spending the night at the House, the Interpreter sets his mark upon them and commands them to dress in white linen before continuing their journey. He also sends his servant Great-heart, with his sword, helmet and shield to conduct them on the next stage. When they come to the place where Christian lost his burden, that is, when they come to the Cross, they pause to praise God, while Great-heart discourses on pardon for sins and justification by faith.

## Commentary

Christiana obviously recalls her indifference to her husband's burden and his desire for peace. At this stage she still fails to understand exactly why he felt the necessity to make the journey, but she also senses not only her wrong towards him but also her need for peace in her own troubled spirit. A letter of personal invitation to go on the journey provides inspiration for her to leave the City of Destruction.

The visit of Secret, the heavenly messenger, which might also be viewed as the Holy Spirit, sets Christiana on her way.

From the first she has to reckon with tempters, who are quick to remind her of the hardships of the way, especially seen, the tempters suggest, by those with good minds. For Christiana as for Christian, however, there is only one way – the way of the Cross. Prior to the pardon which they will receive at the Cross, the pilgrims see the scenes which Christian saw – 'The Significant Room' of the House of the Spirit.

The sense of mystery is not as evident as in Part One, for there are the familiar portraits, and the only new note is the description of the minister's portrait. The pilgrims also see additional tableaux, one of which is 'The Butcher Killing the Sheep', a picture which John Kelman, calls 'one of the ugliest and most revolting things which Bunyan ever wrote'. Kelman is of the opinion that the depiction is closer to Charles II, King of England, than to Christ, the Good Shepherd.

Following instructions in the House of the Spirit, they stop at the Cross, where they recognise, especially from Great-heart's teaching, that Christ placed His righteousness on sinners who repent of sins.

## 2   From the Cross through the Valley of the Shadow of Death

After leaving the Cross, they see Simple, Sloth, and Presumption hanged up in irons, and they hear of those persuaded by these individuals to turn away from a pilgrimage. As they laboriously climb the Hill Difficulty, Great-heart points out the short cuts attempted by Formalist and Hypocrisy in Part One; they climb on until they reach the arbour, where they pause to refresh themselves. Mercy thinks of this spot as a 'losing place', for here Christian lost his 'roll' and Christiana leaves her 'bottle of spirits' behind. One of the boys must return to the arbour to recover the bottle.

Soon the pilgrims come upon a 'stage' bearing a description of the punishment of Timorous and Mistrust, who attempted in Part One to turn Christian back for fear of the lions. They also meet the lions as well as Giant Grim, who now 'backs' the lions and whom Great-heart kills. At the porter's lodge, Great-heart leaves them, since the pilgrims unwisely fail to ask for him as their conductor beyond this point. Then Mr Watchful (the Porter of Part One) asks Christiana about her background, while Humble-mind, a character new in Part

Two, and others prepare dinner. The visitors remain here about a month in order to know Prudence, Piety, and Charity. The people are still the same characters as in Part One, but the House is a noisier place than it was when Christian visited it. Here Prudence asks permission to catechise Christiana's children; at the conclusion, Prudence offers several suggestions, including the need for the boys to hearken to their mother since she will be able 'to learn' them more. During this period, Mercy attracts a suitor, Mr Brisk, a man 'That pretended to Religion; but a man that stuck very close to the World'. When Mr Brisk discovers that Mercy's occupation, making garments for the poor, brings her no money, he breaks off the courtship. The word 'brisk' must have had a rather negative connotation for Bunyan. Readers will recall that Ignorance of Part One was referred to as a 'brisk lad'.

While at the Porter's Lodge, Matthew, one of Christiana's sons, becomes ill from eating fruit from Beelzebub's orchard. Dr Skill's first purge, made of the blood of a goat, the ashes of a heifer and juices of hyssop, offers no relief. Only a purging from 'the body and blood of Christ' proves effective in treating Matthew's illness. Following his healing, Matthew becomes unusually interested in asking Prudence numerous questions – most of them stupid – regarding the cleansing of the body, heart and mind and on other matters pertaining to his understanding of God's work in the world.

After almost a month at the House Beautiful, the pilgrims realise that they must continue their journey. Joseph, another of Christiana's sons, reminds his mother to send the Interpreter a request for the services of Great-heart. The hosts recognise that the travellers should go on their way, and they call the 'whole House' together to give thanks for sending them these guests. They then show the pilgrims particular objects on which to meditate as they travel: one of the apples of Eve, Jacob's ladder, a golden anchor, and the mountain upon which Abraham offered up Isaac, along with the altar, the wood, the fire and the knife. Prudence then plays upon a pair of 'Excellent Virginals' and sings for them. Great-heart returns with wine and food. The Porter gives them information about the King's highway, blesses the pilgrims, and receives a 'Gold Angel' from Christiana.

As they are about to depart, Piety suddenly remembers that she had forgotten to give something she had intended for Christiana.

While they wait for Piety's return, Prudence explains to Christiana the 'curious' notes of the country birds when flowers appear in the spring. By this time, Piety has come back with a 'Scheme' of all the emblems they have seen at the House Beautiful. Christiana may look upon these things for her edification and comfort.

The pilgrims now go down to the 'Hill into the Valley of Humiliation', a valley in sharp contrast to what Christian found it to be. The beauty of the description appears to be more like the land of Beulah than the Valley of Humiliation, and the prose is some of the most exquisite in the whole of Part Two. In the Valley, the travellers find a monument erected to the memory of Christian's fight with Apollyon and they discover a pillar describing Christian's 'slips'. They also pass a shepherd boy feeding his father's sheep and singing a song. But when the pilgrims reach the Valley of the Shadow of Death it is an unsettling experience for all of them. They hear groans; they smell loathsome odours; one of the boys becomes ill, and they feel the ground shake beneath them. Darkness issues from a pit; they see Heedless lying in a ditch, and they ponder the wonder of Christian's escape from the numerous snares on every side.

*Commentary*

The House Beautiful seems to be a place primarily for training and teaching in spiritual matters. Prudence does most of the teaching, but later permits the sons of Christiana to ask questions. What is revealed by these question–answer sessions is primarily that the natural world is a teacher as well as the Bible. The House Beautiful is also a place of relaxation and fellowship for this group of Christian pilgrims.

The objects on which the travellers are to reflect as they go on in the way are slightly perplexing. Eve's apple, for example, appears to suggest not only what can possibly follow for the one who looks on sin but also the possibility that the desire to know can lead to doubt. Christiana is unsure whether the apple is 'Food or Poyson'. Another object, Jacob's ladder, shows a connection between earth and heaven, and Christ established that fundamental connection in his Incarnation. The golden anchor of hope, which the pilgrims are told to carry with them, is particularly perplexing. There are several possible explanations, but what is beyond question is a reference to hope as an anchor – a stabilising quality – for the Christian traveller. What one sees in the sacrifice of Abraham is certainly, in part, the need for a love for God which is so intense that it must include self-denial. There seems also to be an emphasis on this quality of love as characteristic of the pilgrim from the earliest eras of Biblical history.

The Valley of Humiliation, depicted so contrastingly with the same valley where Christian fought with Apollyon, is now a place of beauty. In this valley, Christian fought one of his most violent battles, but for Christiana and her companions it becomes a place of pleasant sojourn. It is also a 'fruitful place' beautiful 'with Lillies'. Yet as the monument to Christian's battle indicates, it is important for the Christian pilgrim to remember the strong spiritual virtues of those who preceded him. Following the incredible beauty of the Valley of Humiliation, the travellers come to the ghastly ugliness of the Valley of the Shadow of Death. Sounds and smells are almost intolerable. What seems apparent is the realistic and morbid predicament of the soul facing the horrors of various temptations.

## 3   From the Valley of the Shadow of Death through Vanity Fair

The Pilgrims now come to the cave of Giant Maul whom Great-heart slays. As a warning for others who might follow, they set up a pillar with an account of their experiences there and mount the giant's head on the top. Then they rest at the spot where Christian first saw Faithful. Under an oak tree, they find an old pilgrim, Honest. He hesitates to give his name and blushes when Great-heart recognises him. They exchange stories of other pilgrims, the weak and the self-willed.

As the pilgrims progress, events develop rapidly. They meet Gaius, an Innkeeper, who provides for their entertainment, talks of Christian's ancestors, advises Christiana to get her children married so that her husband's name will survive, and delivers a discourse on women. During this stay, the adults talk and tell riddles; Gaius, Great-heart and Honest attack Slay-good, and Great-heart cuts off the giant's head and rescues Feeble-mind. Matthew marries Mercy; John marries Phoebe, the daughter of Gaius; and all take part in feastings.

When the pilgrims continue their journey, the next stop is Vanity Fair where they stay with old Mnason who requests his daughter, Grace, to invite other good men of the town to meet the pilgrims. Persecutions rarely occur now in Vanity Fair, but weddings continue to be on the minds of the pilgrims. Samuel, Christiana's son, marries

Grace; and another of her sons, Joseph, marries Grace's sister, Martha. Bunyan does not permit his travellers to be unmindful of Faithful's suffering and death in Vanity Fair (in Part One), for they pause at the place where Faithful died and offer thanks to God for enabling Faithful to bear his cross so well.

*Commentary*
Giant Maul undoubtedly has some relationship to religious and legal authority, but Great-heart overcomes this powerful giant. After the victory there follows a brief period of rest, conversation and rejoicing. Several weak pilgrims receive mention; this reminds readers of the need for compassion for those of weak or little faith.

Old Honest is, as his name suggests, a straightforward man. His long speeches show little imagination, but his plain statements are without ambiguity. It is through Old Honest that the author makes his memorable descriptions of Fearing and Self-will.

Vanity Fair is seen in sharp contrast to the depiction of this town in Part One. Here it is primarily a place for conversation and socialising. The pilgrims become acquainted with many people of the Fair, and there are among these natives several individuals capable of showing kind acts of human concern. Apparently Bunyan wishes to suggest that not all people living in Vanity Fair are persecutors of Christian pilgrims.

**4   From Vanity Fair to the Land of Beulah**

After leaving Vanity Fair, they pass the Hill Lucre and come to the river before the Delectable Mountains. They even find a baby-sitter for Christiana's grandchildren. The men go to Doubting Castle, kill Giant Despair's wife, and later march against Despair and cut off his head. Following a celebration with music and dancing, they now come to the Delectable Mountains where they see the sights which the shepherds showed Christian, combined with new scenes on Mounts Marvel, Innocent and Charity. It is on the Delectable Mountains that Mercy, now pregnant, asks for a 'looking glass' hanging in the shepherds' dining room – an incident on which numerous Bunyan scholars spill ink.

As the singing pilgrims depart, they meet Valiant-for-truth and soon arrive at the Enchanted Ground where they encounter near-impenetrable darkness. So difficult is the way that Great-heart takes out a map (probably the Bible) to find clear direction. Soon they see a man on his knees: Mr Stand-fast, who is in a position of prayer in order to stay the attacks from a Mrs Bubble whom Bunyan describes as wearing a great purse at her side.

Finally, Beulah, that beautiful land of their 'marriage with Christ', receives them with trumpets sounding and bells ringing. In this glorious land the pilgrims await 'the good Hour' of death. Christiana is the first to receive the summons to the Celestial City and she enters in 'at the Gate with all the Ceremonies of Joy that her Husband *Christian* had done before her'. Death comes, in turn, to other pilgrims, each of whom delivers final words, as did Christiana, before they cross the river.

The narrator does not stay to witness Christiana's children and grandchildren crossing over the river, but he simply says that, if he passes that way again, he may give 'those that desire it' an account of what he is here 'silent about'.

## Commentary

The Hill Lucre or the temptation to become rich offers no allurement for Christiana and her companions. These pilgrims have all they need; they have a deep satisfaction, but their peace does not come from material possessions.

Diffidence, the wife of Giant Despair, and one who is not necessarily an honest doubter but one who is simply indifferent to faith, meets her death. Her lethargy is not honest and sincere doubting; consequently, her indifference can be destroyed by straightforward, honest treatment. It is appropriate that Honest kills Diffidence, but it is equally appropriate for Great-heart, not Honest, to kill Despair, this hard-hearted creature who has been destroying untold numbers for years. His influence still extends to people like Despondency and Much-afraid, but the fact that these individuals are not yet Despair's victims gives cause for rejoicing among the pilgrims.

On the Delectable Mountains the beauty of the landscape is not nearly so clearly depicted as in Part One, but, as in Part One, the mountains are places for new spiritual insight and understanding; however, it is the weak pilgrim, not the strong, who here receives special concern.

Pilgrims along the way, like Valiant-for-Truth and Stand-fast, are important aspects of the Christian pilgrimage. They are strong men: Valiant is a courageous warrior; Stand-fast is a pilgrim in constant prayer, and both are able to withstand the enchanting allurement of the flesh and the devil.

What receives clear emphasis at the end is the lack of grimness or morbidity in death. Zestfulness characterises the life of the strong pilgrim; dying evidences the same spirit. Christian pilgrims happily receive their summons to the new city.

48

# 6 THEMES AND ISSUES

## 6.1  THE COMMON JOURNEY OF ALL CHRISTIANS

The meeting of Christian and Hopeful with the shepherds of the
Delectable Mountains leads to an illuminating but ambiguous conversation among them. The conversation suggests two fundamental
senses of the metaphor of the way, a metaphor which Bunyan
appropriates scores of times in the allegory. One sense of the
metaphor is obviously the way all pilgrims must take if they earnestly
desire to enter the Celestial City. That there is this sense of the
metaphor and yet another sense appears certain from the following
conversation:

> CHR. Is this the way to the Celestial City?
> SHEP. You are just in your way.
> CHR. *How far is it thither?*
> SHEP. Too far for any, but those that *shall* get
> thither indeed.
> CHR. *Is the way safe, or dangerous?*
> SHEP. Safe for those for whom it is to be safe,
> *but transgressors shall fall therein.* (pp. 97–8)

There is, then, one common journey for all pilgrims and that way,
which they *must* go, usually includes every major stage which
Christian travels. But no questing pilgrim can make the journey
without going through the Wicket-Gate and without stopping at the
Cross. This is the way he must go. The shepherds underscore the
convictions of Christian and Hopeful, as well as Faithful, that there is

the one true way to the Celestial City. Yet, as we shall see, there is an additional consideration, and to appreciate the nature of his devotion to the metaphor of the way one *must* go, the reader should recognise that Bunyan uses this figure of 'the way' in two senses.

## 6.2  THE INDIVIDUAL PATHWAY

Another sense of the metaphor of the way is the questing, demonstrable, inner faith of each pilgrim. This inner faith includes an earnest desire to leave the City of Destruction and to travel the way that leads to the Celestial City. This faith also includes a strong belief that there *is* a way to the new city, and the believer who has faith in the Christ of the Cross will attain the goal. To suggest that faith is never vulnerable to doubt is not Bunyan's thinking. Christian's greatest moment of doubt comes when he is far along in his pilgrimage; in fact, doubt plagues him to the very end of the journey.

Furthermore, even one of little faith may be in the true way and yet lack the strength of some pilgrims. The character, Little-faith, whom Christian and Hopeful meet, is not a great man or hero, but his small faith does not debar him from being in the way he *must* go. To ignore faith, as Ignorance does, or to disdain it as does Atheist is to miss the way one must go. There is room for variety and diversity among individual pilgrims on the common journey, but the way from the City of Destruction to the Celestial City has no place for anyone who is impervious to faith.

The need for faith runs like a thread throughout the allegory. In the early stages of the journey the pilgrim has to learn that faith is not the same as having worldly wisdom (Wordly Wiseman) or keeping the law (Mr Legality), or doing good works (The Village of Morality). At the Cross, Christian is justified by faith in Christ. His 'rags' are removed and new clothes, suggesting the new man, replace them. When he sleeps and loses his parchment roll, he learns early that faith requires vigilance; he exercises faith when he refuses to turn away from the lions, he finds nurture for his faith in the Interpreter's House and the House Beautiful, but he also discovers that faith must never be equated with overconfidence and that faith needs constant nourishment.

It is also by faith alone that the pilgrims from the hill Clear see the place 'hoped for' through the shepherds' perspective glass. Lack of faith can – and must – be overcome even at the moment of death if one is to enter the glorious Celestial City.

In studying *The Pilgrim's Progress* readers will observe numerous references to 'the way', but an awareness of the sense in which the author uses the term is essential to understanding the allegory. Clearly then, the way is the path of all Christians from this world to the Celestial City, but it is also the way of faith of the individual. The way for all Christians includes stopping at the Interpreter's House, falling at the Cross, entering the House Beautiful and, simultaneously, enduring the struggles and temptations, but facing these with a spiritual armour such as Christian received at the House Beautiful.

On the other hand, an individual is only in 'the way' if he acknowledges that he is a sinner and accepts by faith Christ's sacrificial death and the righteousness which He provides. It is important to hear Scriptural outlines which provide a map of the journey from the City of Destruction to the Celestial City, but the experience of the journey can never be known unless the individual senses a personal need to travel it himself. Bunyan insists on the way one 'must go', but a cursory glance at the conversation on shared experiences between Hopeful and Christian, for example, clearly indicates that believers' experiences in the Way may differ. Briefly, there is only one way – the way of the cross – for any person to become a Christian pilgrim, but once one is in the way, experiences of Christian pilgrims may not be identical to those of Christian, Faithful and Hopeful.

Reference to 'the way' contained in *The Pilgrim's Progress*, as well as allusions to those in it, those who talk about it, those who take short cuts around it, and those who ignore it will provide a rich and provocative study for the careful reader.

## 6.3 THE NATURE OF TEMPTATION

From the beginning to the end of the journey, Christian is confronted with varieties of temptations. Perhaps the order in which they appear is not particularly important, but assaults come from family, neighbours, would-be friends, fiends, enemies, individuals and society. It is obvious, however, that the most violent temptations come comparatively early in Christian's journey – that of Apollyon, for example, soon after he has put on his spiritual armour. Following the fierce battle with Apollyon in the Valley of Humiliation, he struggles successfully against the fiends of the Valley of the Shadow, only to encounter (after a brief interlude) the hostile society of Vanity Fair. Early temptations are deliberate, overt and violent. Later ones come in the form of deception and complacency. Demas and Flatterer seek to deceive, but the pilgrims are not sufficiently alert to the dangers of By-Path meadow and the Enchanted Ground. (Admittedly, Christian appears to understand far better than Hopeful the perils of the Enchanted Ground.)

What is particularly clear in a study of these various temptations is that they may come in some form at any stage of Christian's journey. Even though Christian grows in understanding of the way he must go, he still faces horrible temptations almost at the close of the journey, and especially notable are those of Doubting Castle and The River of Death. In localising the terrors and describing the pervasiveness of temptation, Bunyan shows with unmistakable clarity that temptations can be met in triumph and that they never permanently overcome the pilgrim. The Book in the pilgrim's hand, the teaching by the Interpreter, the fellowship in the House Beautiful, the meeting with the shepherds, and the companionship of fellow believers are powerful bulwarks against temptation.

# 7 TECHNICAL FEATURES

## 7.1  SIGHT AND AURAL SENSE

Bunyan gives a prominent emphasis to the visual and aural senses in his allegory. At the beginning, when Christian meets Evangelist and tells him of the heavy burden on his back, Evangelist responds in a scene crucial to an understanding of *The Pilgrim's Progress*. This scene is worthy of much study, for it immediately establishes two ways of seeing:

> Then said *Evangelist*, pointing
> with his finger over a very wide
> Field, Do you see yonder *Wicket-*
> *gate*? The Man said, No. Then
> said the other, Do you see yonder
> shining light? He said, I think I
> do. Then said *Evangelist*, Keep that
> light in your eye, and go up
> directly thereto, so shalt thou see
> that Gate; at which when thou
> knockest, it shall be told thee
> what thou shalt do.
> So I saw in my Dream, that the
> Man began to run; Now he had not
> run far from his own door, but his
> Wife and Children perceiving it,
> began to cry after him to return;
> but the Man put his fingers in his

Ears, and ran on crying, Life, Life,
Eternal Life: so he looked not
behind him, but fled towards the
middle of the Plain. (pp. 9–10)

On the surface, the selected scene seems to indicate that someone
who is aware of accurate directions is giving such directions in a
precise manner to a traveller. What is here is one of the earliest of
Bunyan's metaphorical passages as well as a hint that seeing concrete,
literal details is seeing only in part. To ignore seeing more than the
literal, we know by this time, is to miss the allegory.

Evangelist sees 'yonder *Wicket-gate*', and understands why it is
important to see it. At first the would-be pilgrim categorically denies
that he sees it. When Evangelist immediately speaks of 'yonder
shining light', the pilgrim falters and replies that he thinks he sees it.
Apparently Evangelist sees a light – a light of faith – in the pilgrim's
eyes, for he tells him that he will see 'the Gate' if he keeps that light
in his eyes. The narrator and the reader see a man beginning to run;
the wife and children perceive or *see* a man running from them.
Undoubtedly the running man sees something, or thinks he sees
something, beyond actual time and space. He refuses to look back
and he cries out, 'Life, Life, Eternal Life'.

It is evident that seeing only on the visible level is a troubling
temptation for Christian in the initial stages of the pilgrimage, as well
as an all-too-frequent problem throughout his journey. Convinced by
Mr Worldly Wiseman that he must find Legality to get on the right
route, Christian asks of him the way:

> CHR. Sir, which is my way to this
> honest man's house?
> WORL. *Do you see yonder high hill?*
> CHR. Yes, very well.
> WORL. By that *Hill* you must go, and
> the first house you come to
> is his. (p. 16)

This blundering pilgrim, who has barely finished saying he thinks he
sees 'yonder shining light' is now positive that he sees 'very well' the
way to Mr Legality's house up 'yonder high hill'. He sees clearly on
one level, but the Gate is beyond the literal level, and he appears

unable to see the invisible. Only with the help of Evangelist does Christian see his error and begin to see again on the level of the invisible.

References to seeing flood the work. When he attempts to convince Pliable to accompany him on his journey, Christian says ' . . . there we shall see the Elders with their Golden Crowns: There we shall see the Holy Virgins with their Golden Harps' (p. 12). After a lengthy catalogue of things and human beings and angels to *see*, Pliable makes the reader aware of the aural sense when he replies: '*The hearing of this is enough to ravish ones heart*' (p. 12).

In many passages the visual and aural combine. When the narrator speaks of Christian's combat with Apollyon, he says in part, ' . . . no man can imagine, unless he had seen and heard as I did, what yelling, and hideous roaring *Apollyon* made . . . and on the other side what sighs and groans brast from *Christians* heart. I never saw him all the while give so much as one pleasant look . . . ' (p. 49).

Although his use of the visual and aural abound throughout the work, Bunyan, in the final analysis, juxtaposes the two senses: one has to see and hear if the joys and perils of the journey are to be understood. When Christian 'thinks' he sees (in the passage quoted), almost simultaneously he refuses to hear the calls of his family and neighbours by placing his fingers in his ears. Along the way, the Interpreter (in the Interpreter's House) nourishes Christian's sight; so also do people like Prudence, Charity and Piety, especially through their counsel, nurture the aural sense. Conversations with the shepherds nourish the aural and the visual senses. Whether Bunyan places the emphasis on visual or aural separately or in juxtaposition, he expects the individual to perceive beyond the mere sights and sounds to the complex meanings of both. The literal level of either sense is not sufficient.

It is surely appropriate, however, that the Celestial City comes to Christian and Hopeful through the two senses. See and hear the following: 'And now were these two men, as 'twere, in Heaven, before they came at it; being swallowed up with the sight of Angels, and with hearing of their melodious notes. Here also they had the City it self in view, and they thought they heard all the Bells therein to ring, to welcome them thereto . . . ' (p. 131).

## 7.2  REALISM

Author and critic C. S. Lewis once stated that everything 'is
visualized in terms of the contemporary life that Bunyan knew'. The
objects that Pilgrim meets on the journey are homely details: a
quagmire, the highway, roads without signposts, bypaths and short
cuts through pleasant meadows, steep hills and dark valleys, an inn,
gardens and orchards, the town fair on market day; the river that
must be crossed. Such observable objects have the immediacy of
daily experience. The realism is also evident in the perilous nature of
the pilgrim's journey, with the presence of giants, wild beasts,
hobgoblins, and robbers. Equally strong realism appears in the
various conversations among the travellers on the journey: Christian
and Faithful compare notes on their divers experiences in their
pilgrimage, By-ends tells Christian about his family and his
background, Christian and Hopeful discuss the road ahead and argue
over which is the better route, and Christian and Faithful discuss
Talkative's character until Christian convinces Faithful that a 'talker'
and a 'doer' are not identical.

If conversation depicts Bunyan's realism, so also does the dominant characteristic he gives to characters. In only a few words he is
able to pinpoint the essential nature of a character, as with his
reference to Ignorance as 'a very brisk lad', or to Talkative 'whose
religion is only in word', or Atheist's 'very great laughter'. His
engaging realism is not only important in showing his shrewd
observations of people, but also in demonstrating the significance of
what he observes. For Bunyan there is some spiritual meaning in
every object, every action and every feeling.

Equally realistic are his colloquial expressions. He refers to two
men who come 'tumbling over the wall', to Apollyon who 'strodled'
quite over the whole breadth of the way, to a 'little crooked lane'
where there appears Ignorance, and to the lock in Doubting Castle
that 'went damnable hard'. Unsophisticated expressions are crucial
aspects of Bunyan's natural style and language, a language which
James Sutherland, a scholar of English Literature, perceives as
'concerned always with getting the thing said'.

## 7.3  DIALOGUE

Dialogue and narrative closely interweave throughout the allegory. In referring to this characteristic, an outstanding Bunyan scholar, Henri Talon, states: 'In all these pages dialogues knot and unknot themselves with a curious virtuosity. And in the centre Christian dominates always, keeping the unity of the work intact.'

That Bunyan had thought about dialogue as a literary tool is evident from his rhymed preface. 'I find that men (as high as Trees) will write Dialogue-wise', he states, and his allegory abounds in dialogue. The dialogue between Christian and Mr Worldly Wiseman is especially excellent. In only a few paragraphs the author shows through dialogue the self-satisfaction of Worldly Wiseman with his contempt for Christian's idea of the way he says he must go. Equally contemptuous are his charges that Evangelist's counsel is unsound and that Christian's willingness to follow such advice arises from a weak intellect. At the same time the dialogue reveals a vivid picture of Christian: he is sincere in his conviction that he is on the right route to the new city, but he is not quite prepared for Wiseman's insidious comments. The latter's first remarks to the pilgrim indicate his cunning manner: *'How now, good fellow, whither away after this burdened manner?'* When Christian tells him that, on Evangelist's counsel, he is going to the Wicket-gate to 'be put into a way' to get rid of his burden, Wiseman taunts him by saying, 'There is not a more dangerous and troublesome way in the world, than is that into which he hath directed thee' (p. 15). To entrap Christian further, Wiseman speaks as though he has the best interest of Christian at heart, and knowingly tells him that what troubles him also upsets other weak men 'who meddle with things too high for them'. Christian is nervous and uncomfortable in the presence of this man of worldly reputation who seemingly speaks with authority. This view of Christian reveals a position typical of John Bunyan throughout the allegory: faith frequently coexists with weakness.

For a vivid depiction of the 'terse manageableness' (to use George Bernard Shaw's term) and of the vivid directness of statements, the entire dialogue between Obstinate and Christian is without equal. Notice the way in which Obstinate begins each sentence: 'What! . . . leave our Friends, and our Comforts behind us!'; 'Tush . . . away with your Book', and 'What! more Fools still?' (p. 10–11) Obstinate is the kind of person who knows answers even before he knows the questions. No one can reason with him; even if one counsels him, he hears nothing, and even if he does hear, he has already made up his mind on any subject and has no plans to change. Obstinate's remarks ring with finality, and never will he open his closed mind to any new knowledge. He thinks he needs no help from either people or books; he also makes intimidating and condescending assertions to any individual who dares to challenge his point of view or seems to lack interest in his ill-advised opinions. However, Christian's terse and direct responses show a person resolute of purpose, showing little interest in following Obstinate's pseudo-reasoning. He simply responds to Obstinate by saying, 'I have laid my hands to the Plow.' Equally terse is the reply of Obstinate as he watches Pliable and Christian depart: 'And I will go back to my place . . . I will be no Companion of such mis-led fantastical Fellows.' (p. 11)

If Bunyan uses dialogue to explore encounters between human beings, so similarly he appropriates it to show states of mind. The experiences of Christian and Hopeful in Doubting Castle clearly reveal states of mind. Motivated by vain confidence, Christian persuades Hopeful to follow him along a strange route – one, the pilgrims later discover, which leads them to property belonging to the Giant Despair. After Giant Despair throws them into a dark dungeon and beats them, the pilgrims sink into a state of relentless hopelessness. They are now miserable pilgrims, and their misery comes not exclusively from the brutal persecutions of Giant Despair. They know that they are at fault for even coming near Doubting Castle. Furthermore, Giant Despair's beating 'without mercy' of the two pilgrims is primarily a torturing and beating of their minds and spirits which they painfully experience.

No reader should overlook the interior dialogue in the episode of the Valley of the Shadow of Death. The horrible battle here is Christian's inward battle of indecision. Without question, Bunyan emphasises the dangers of the valley: on the right is a deep ditch; on the left is a dangerous quagmire; the pathway is narrow, the darkness is almost blinding, and the sounds of 'doleful voices' are terrifying. An examination of the episode might suggest on the surface that Christian is attempting to reason about his situation and to draw near a conclusion. Closer scrutiny shows that the inner dialogue shifts ground every few seconds (see the 'yet' and 'but' and 'then') and Christian wages a tumultuous battle with irresolution.

## 7.4  CHARACTERISATION

The principal characters are, of course, Christian, Faithful, and
Hopeful. Some modern readers make the point that Bunyan's
characters generally have adjectives rather than nouns for names.
Christian's major fellow travellers are 'Faithful', not 'Faith', and
'Hopeful', not 'Hope'. To see the characters only as types can inhibit
the reader from seeing the symbolic function of the literal name.
Certainly Bunyan's characters do have a symbolic function, even
though they do frequently exemplify particular qualities or conditions. It can also be argued that the author frequently pares down a
character to his most distinguishing trait, such as Ignorance's
'briskness', but Bunyan does not completely subsume any human
being within one adjectival characteristic. No 'name tag' so inflexibly
predetermines individuals that they become only rigid, fixed
examples of a particular virtue.

What a reader especially notices in the main character, *Christian*, is
not simply his strong qualities as a Christian and as the hero of the
work, but also his numerous human weaknesses. In his symbolic
function, the exemplifier of Christians of all eras from their conversion at the Cross through their growth in grace, and through every
stage of the warfare between the spirit and the flesh until they
reach the Celestial City, Christian makes his share of errors; he
also demonstrates courage, perseverance and faith.

In the beginning, Christian is a restless individual with 'a book in
hand, and a great burden on his back'. He is sensitive to the
injunctions of the book and to the limitations of his own ability.
When Evangelist suddenly appears, to ask why Christian laments, he
answers, 'Sir, I perceive, by the Book in my hand, that I am
Condemned to die, and after that to come to Judgment; and I find
that I am not willing to do the first, nor able to do the second' (p. 9).
As this scene signals, whatever Christian does or becomes is very
much bound up with that book in his hand. Thus, in his restlessness,
he listens to one who understands the directions embodied in that
book.

So the troubled, restless, burdened man begins with passionate
zeal a long journey. Restlessness, springing from fear of judgement,
drops off at the Cross. But before he arrives at the Cross, he strays
from the path he must go, primarily because he experiences an
unexpected attack on his intelligence and understanding from

Worldly-Wiseman. Prior to the meeting with this man of the world, Christian shows will and determination even though he falls into the 'Slough of Dispond'.

Struggles, battles and hardships contribute to his spiritual health. Lions, giants and monsters fail to tempt him; in fact, they intensify his courage and strengthen his will. As Talon says of Christian, ' . . . he finds peace of soul only in the tumult of battle, forgetting danger in the moment of facing it'. Lack of peace does come, however, at least twice: in Doubting Castle he sinks almost into complete despair, and at the River of Death 'a great horror and darkness' fall upon him.

Christian is also a perceptive man. He has insight into human personality. Talkative is no surprise for him, and he is sure that he knows Talkative better than he knows himself, even though this pretender is able to talk 'pilgrim language'. Christian is so perceptive and argues with such precision that his friend, Hopeful, thinks of him as learned. Certainly he can be a friendly, even a gentle person with his comrades Faithful and Hopeful and, to a great extent, to one like Little-Faith, but he can be stern and severe with pretenders like Formalist or Talkative.

On the other hand, he can be complacent and lose his roll in the Arbour and he can seek a short cut and stray around in By-Path Meadow. Almost at the end of his journey, he is still capable of falling into the 'net of Flattery'. Although fear of judgement falls off at the Cross, mortal fear of death almost destroys him as he completes the last phase of the journey.

By Christian's side for a distance is *Faithful*, who has courage, but lacks the understanding sensibility of Christian. His temptations lack the violence and ferocity of those Christian confronts. He faces no Apollyon but a Madame Wanton whom he resists, but still has a fleeting happy thought of the delightful wife she might be! Such a thought he soon dismisses by shaking off the temptations of his 'old' or his pre-Christian nature. He appears to enjoy telling Christian of his encounter with creatures called Discontent and Shame and his victory over these tempters. This is not meant to suggest that Faithful attempts to be priggish or to appear manly, for much respect is due to one who overcomes a grumbling spirit. It should also be remembered that Faithful, a Puritan, perhaps frequently encounters ridicule and laughter from others in society, and he surely does in Vanity Fair. To be treated as one who has no claim to respect, who is a victim of caricature and is yet able to remain undaunted is a victory deserving some notice. Obviously Faith is the absolute essential in the conflict with Shame.

There is a consistency in Faithful's attitude toward Shame, particularly graphic in the scene with Christian at Vanity Fair. At this place where the garments and speech of the pilgrims become the butt of sarcasm, Faithful (and Christian) show heroic courage and faithfulness. Even unto death, Faithful is the exemplar of a steadfast spirit, and his commitment makes a profound impact, certainly on one man, Hopeful. Through Faithful's death, Hopeful awakens to a desire for the Christian Way.

Before looking more closely at *Hopeful*, two remarks from Talon seem appropriate: 'Hopeful is a ghost among richly vital characters' and he is made up of 'bits and pieces ill joined together'. He is far less colourful than Faithful and Christian and even less interesting than several minor characters. Christian certainly overshadows Hopeful and surely snubs him on occasion, but Hopeful encourages Christian in one of his most terrifying experiences. He is no mean thinker in dialogue with Christian and adds a dimension to the reader's understanding of Faithful's bout with Shame. In Hopeful's opinion, some backslide because of what they consider the 'shame that attends Religion', for religion 'in their eyes is low and contemptible'. Although he is not on the same scale as Christian or Faithful, Hopeful is a cheerful, pleasant person. Christianity, for him, as we might expect, is full of hope for the true pilgrim.

If we view the principal characters not as mere types but as individuals with symbolic functions, so also must we observe that although minor characters, too, exemplify particular qualities, they are still personalities not completely absorbed by one attribute.

The first major temptation which Christian confronts is offered by *Mr Worldly-Wiseman*. He speaks with such authority that he impresses Christian as someone who must know everything that is worth knowing. Not only is he particularly omniscient, but he wants to share his knowledge. He freely gives advice on subjects ranging from the beliefs any intelligent person ought to hold to the village where any prudent person ought to live. To add to his authority and stature, he stays away from the thinking of 'weak men' who meddle in things too high for them, as when reading the Bible. What Worldly-Wiseman symbolises is the legalistic individual who thinks he can win his own salvation by keeping the law of Moses. While he observes his own religion, he will at the same time enjoy freely the wise insights which the world offers. He has no need for a special Book. To live 'near' the village of Morality is sufficient for him. Mr Worldly-Wiseman's depiction is brief, but one of Bunyan's most graphically drawn.

The antithesis of Worldly-Wiseman is *Evangelist*. He appears to Christian before and after his encounter with Worldly-Wiseman. When Evangelist first appears he comes with merciful pardon contained in the parchment roll, and instructs Christian clearly, factually and simply. He says no more than is essential, and his questions are squarely on target. His primary effect on Christian is to lead him to see the truth about himself and his deepest need. To help him to find a solution to his plight, Evangelist gives directions to a wicket gate, which Christian, at this stage, is unable to see clearly.

Following Christian's meeting with Worldly-Wiseman, Evangelist makes a second appearance. He comes to meet the pilgrim and asks sharp, pointed questions. With weighed words, he chides Christian for his actions, and he does so by showing him the words of God. So piercing are the words that Christian falls down at the feet of Evangelist.

Evangelist helps get the action of the story going but plays no direct part in it. He makes his final appearance to Christian and Faithful and foretells their suffering in Vanity Fair and their happiness in the new City.

One of Bunyan's most intriguing minor characters is *Talkative*. One needs more than a dictionary definition in order to appreciate the significance of Bunyan's Talkative, an understanding of whom can be drawn only on the basis of the author's own portrayal. Close observation shows that Talkative is a living personality who obviously enjoys talking, and if talking were the crucial mark of the Christian pilgrim, then Talkative would be no less a pilgrim than Christian or Faithful or Hopeful. This shallow man from Prating Row can *talk* on any conceivable subject, and to talk is 'most profitable', according to him. By talking, 'a Man may get knowledge of many things; as of the vanity of earthly things . . . learn the necessity of the New-birth, the insufficiency of our works, the need of Christs righteousness' (p. 63). And if we believe him, the subjects on which he is able to talk are endless: 'things heavenly, or things earthly; things Moral, or things Evangelical; things Sacred, or things Prophane; things past, or things to come; things forraign, or things at home; Essential, or things Circumstantial' (p. 63).

Obviously, few matters are beyond Talkative's comprehension, or so he thinks. His conversation with Faithful reveals that he mistakes words for reality: he is pretentious and theatrical and seeks to hide from the truth and from God in his word-built world. He can talk, and he surely does, but he cannot *be* and, as a result, he cannot *do*. Talkative does not fool Christian with his wordiness; he sees through the frothiness of his endless chatter. By transferring the attribute of talkative as an abstract quality into a dramatic depiction of a living personality, Bunyan clearly shows that he does more than interject types into his allegory. By having this verbose man encounter other men, the author demonstrates the nature of his Talkative, lets him catch himself in his own web and, at the same time, reveals the difference between the true pilgrim and the one who simply talks the language of a pilgrim. He also ties a quality or attribute and a living person to his dominant metaphor, a man on a pilgrimage.

It is true, of course, that the names Bunyan gives to his characters are appropriate. This is not only true of Talkative but of each personality. Obstinate is a closed-minded, stubborn individual who begins almost every sentence with an exclamation. His mind is made up; he desires no further information than what he thinks he has. Timorous and Mistrust are afraid to proceed on their pilgrimage; yet, all four people, Talkative, Obstinate, Timorous and Mistrust, are pilgrims, temporary, false, ill-advised, but pilgrims whom Christian encounters on his journey.

Apparently fascinated by names, Bunyan frequently makes his distinctions by giving, as well as the name of the characters, the name of the hometown and the name of relatives. When Christian meets Mr By-ends, for example, By-ends hesitates to reveal his name, which is a strong indication that he prefers not to be recognised. Bunyan just lets him talk and before he utters many words, it becomes clear that he is from the town of Fair-speech, largely inhabited by his relatives, with names such as Lord Turn-about, Lord Time-server, Mr Facing-both-ways and other revealing nomenclatures. He also has connections with the parson, Mr Two-tongues. Bunyan's humour abounds as By-ends alerts the reader to his status. He is also a man with such lack of purpose about a pilgrimage that this pseudo-pilgrim hardly realises what he actually reveals of himself. By-ends says, for example, "'Tis true, we somewhat differ in religion from those of stricter sort, yet but in two small points: First, we never strive against Wind and Tide. Secondly, we are always most zealous when Religion goes in his Silver Slippers; we love much to walk with him in the street, if the Sun shines, and the people applaud it' (p. 81). What a picture of a hypocrite! He seems completely unaware of how hypocritical he actually is, but the reader is not fooled, for his words are like a mirror, reflecting an exact image of him.

*The Pilgrim's Progress* literally teems with characters. A reader meets them in ones and twos, sometimes several individuals together, but each one clearly differentiated.

Few characters, if any, in the Second Part are as fully drawn or as complex as those of the popular Part One, but attention should be focused on a number of them.

*Christiana* is a sensitive woman, and the memory of her good husband, Christian, setting out alone on his pilgrimage, frequently arouses her emotions. As she meditates on the urgency of Christian's words when he departs on his journey, she senses her own need to follow in his steps. She appears to be an intelligent woman, and the Interpreter refers to her as 'a Woman quick of apprehension'. Her acute awareness of the incongruity between inner conditions of the heart and outward 'signs' of following in the Christian way is also evident. In dealing with her children, she is persuasive, loving and affectionate. When circumstances demand it, she can strike against her adversaries, and frequently courage is a primary characteristic of this somewhat vivacious woman. Given the quality of guidance which Christiana has throughout her pilgrimage, one can hardly expect her to face the adventures and crises of Christian. Yet it is equally true that she does grow in her faith – and a growing faith within a Christian community is exactly where Bunyan places his emphasis in Part Two. She defies Giant Grim and his lions; she establishes her identity as a true pilgrim; she resolves to walk in the King's highway, and she declares a joyous devotion to Christ when she hears Great-heart's explanation of His sacrifice. With the help of nurturing figures, she becomes a strong Christian pilgrim.

*Mercy* is a true servant, charitable and hard-working. Humility is her constant characteristic, and one of her favourite phrases is 'if I may', which contrasts beautifully with the more confident spirit of Christiana. She is a gentle soul, and Bunyan puts much tenderness into her portrait. Her teasing of her lover, Mr Brisk, indicates that she is not without humour. Her inflammatory remarks regarding Simple, Sloth, and Presumption also suggest that she is capable of being somewhat uncharitable. She says to Great-heart: ' . . . *they shall never be bewailed by me, they have what they deserved and I think it is well that they hang so near the High-way that others may see and take warning*' (p. 177).

Among the women characters, there is one who is definitely an opposite to Christiana and Mercy: the witch, Madam Bubble. Beautifully dressed, she speaks cleverly, smiles continually, constantly wears a purse by her side, and often holds her hand in the purse, 'fingering her money'. Great-heart calls her 'a bold and impudent slut' who will talk 'with any Man'. She laughs pilgrims to scorn but lavishes praise on the rich. This person of 'Swarthy Complexion' is a covetous and lustful older woman.

Additional female characters appear briefly; these include Mrs Timorous, Mrs Bats-eyes, Mrs Inconsiderate, Mrs Know-nothing and Mrs Love-the-flesh. The descriptive names leave no doubt regarding their symbolic function. Mrs Timorous is perhaps the most distinctive of this group. She is a very proper woman to whom little matters except her own short-sighted standards of propriety.

Male pilgrims, both strong and weak, are numerous. Mr Great-heart is a strong guide who is always eager and ready to explain, interpret, or simply to talk. He is a brave man who is equally patient and gentle. To those who are weak in their faith, he shows an extraordinary sensitivity and tenderness, as is evident, for example, in his kindness toward Fearing. He is a man of wide and varied experiences, and even though these experiences have brought special favours into his life, Mr Great-heart does not resort to boastings but rather shows that his work is a result of fulfilment of duty in a spirit of humility.

*Honest* is one of Bunyan's most splendid portraits. He is Old Honest or Father Honest, symbolic of essential qualities of the Christian pilgrim. It is in a vivid scene that Bunyan first presents him, asleep beneath an oak tree (the sturdy oak is appropriate) with his clothes, his staff, and his girdle, all necessary equipment for the Christian pilgrim. He is somewhat defiant when Great-heart awakens him, for he fears that these travellers might possibly be in the company 'of those that some time ago did rob Little-faith of his money'. Reluctant to state his name, he tells Great-heart that he is from the 'Town of Stupidity', which lies 'about four Degrees beyond the City of Destruction'. Later he says his name is Honest, not 'Honesty in the Abstract'. He is a man of insight who speaks candidly and to the point. Generalisations may at times enter his conversations, but concrete particulars more accurately characterise his speech as seen, for example, in his comments on Mr Self-will. In Old Honest's judgement, Self-will is one who cares not for man or argument or example; his special quality is to do only what his mind prompts him to do and nothing more.

Another choice character is Mr Valiant-for-truth. He fights lengthy battles, particularly with theorists, but he is the victor and for the obvious reason that truth is on his side. He teases about the marks of valour that people like Wild-head, Inconsiderate, and Pragmatic leave upon him and admits that these creatures carry away some of his own valour. To ensure triumph in his spiritual warfare, Valiant combines faith in God and belief in the power of the sword of the Spirit, or the Bible, with a strong spirit of his own self-reliance.

*Stand-fast* is another strong pilgrim, introduced near the close of the book. He is a marvellous counterbalance to numerous weak pilgrims who precede him. His portrait is primarily that of a faithful man of prayer with a strong distrust for any whose only apparent appeal is to deter pilgrims. When the summons for his death came, the record reads: '. . . *his Master was not willing that he should be so far from him any longer.*'

A character with physical and moral bravery but little spiritual courage is *Mr Fearing*. This kind of individual seems something of a nuisance to the strong pilgrims. With his contradictions he is, nevertheless, an interesting person. He faces the Hill Difficulty without trouble; he goes down the Valley of Humiliation with ease (admittedly, none had trouble in the Second Part), and he is so serene that he lies down at night and kisses the flowers around him, only to get up at dawn to begin kissing the flowers again. In Vanity Fair, Great-heart thinks Mr Fearing will fight 'with all the men in the Fair', a threatening time that all but turns Great-heart into a Mr Fearing. On the other hand, fear absolutely grips this contradictory man, Mr Fearing, when he thinks on or confronts the state of his spiritual life. He literally roars at the Slough of Despond; he has such a terrifying sense of unworthiness at the gate of Good-will that the latter has to step out to get him if he is to enter; he lies outside the Interpreter's door with tears in his eyes, until Great-heart pleads with him to come inside the house, and when he comes to the River of Death, he truly fears that he will be 'drowned for ever'. However, as Great-heart tells the story of Mr Fearing, he shows that in every troubling incident, there is divine deliverance from all of his needless fears.

*Self-will* is one of those on pilgrimage who simply has no desire to be a strong and good man; he desires to be a pilgrim only in name. He fails to come in at the Wicket-gate but defines his own terms for going on a pilgrimage. Most of all, Self-will is a law unto himself. Mr Feeble-mind, another pilgrim, has hardly any semblance of will; he is weak in body and in mind. What is especially troubling about Feeble-mind is that not only is he obviously feeble but he somewhat enjoys having this distinction, to the extent that those who exercise freedom and judgement offend him. He is a self-pitying, self-conscious and self-centered pilgrim who receives kind treatment and counsel from stronger Christians, especially Great-heart.

Another among the group of weaklings is *Mr Ready-to-hault* who holds his crutches in his hand. Feeble-mind delights in his appearance, for he believes that this character will provide a suitable companion for him. Ready-to-hault shares the delight of Feeble-mind, and shows his pleasure by saying, 'If either my *self*, or my *crutches*, can do thee a pleasure, we are both at thy command, good Mr. *Feeble-mind*.' One of the most delightful pictures of Ready-to-hault shows him sharing the reactions of the true pilgrims at Doubting Castle. The sights of that memorable place call for merriment, particularly for music and dancing. True it is that part of the picture is ghastly, but the cause for rejoicing comes from the realisation that people like Despondency and Much-afraid are still alive and have not been defeated by doubt. This, then, is cause for celebration: Christiana and Mercy play upon the violin and lute, and Ready-to-hault dances with joy; he is unable to dance without 'one Crutch in his Hand', but even with his handicap, 'he footed it well'.

What Bunyan does in his depiction of a rather large group of weak pilgrims is not to glorify their weakness. The emphasis is in the opposite direction: the strong Christian must show a compassionate and caring spirit towards the weaker brother, and towards those who appear to lack essential qualities of Christianity. This trait Christian also exemplified, especially toward Little-faith in Part One.

## 7.5 LANGUAGE AND STYLE

References to the literary features of the preceding sections include observations on Bunyan's style. This section is in one sense a reminder of prior statements as well as additional commentary on the subject. Throughout the study we have insisted that *The Pilgrim's Progress* is allegorical in its wide sweep and in its entirety. Bunyan bases his narrative on a familiar symbol – life as a pilgrimage.

One of the basic distinctions of his allegory is that Bunyan brings the language of prose narrative into contact with the everyday world of human beings. His characters use the speech of ordinary people. His language is simple, and he has at his command proverbs and illustrations associated with ordinary human beings.

Undoubtedly the language is that of seventeenth-century village life. Christian's family believes that 'some frenzy distemper' has got into his head. When he fights with Apollyon, the pilgrim is almost 'pressed to death', and Giant Despair goes after Christian and Hopeful with a good 'crab tree cudgel'. Obstinate's famous exclamation, 'tush!' has a special appeal for the person who finds delight in disagreeing. To call people 'craz'd-headed coxcombs' or 'brain-sick' must also provide satisfying vocabulary for the Obstinates of the world. The provincial speech of Little-faith after the experience of the highway robbery is memorable: 'Now after a while, *Little-faith* came to himself, and getting up, made shift to scrabble on his way.' (p. 103)

To appropriate proverbs and make them his own is also characteristic of Bunyan's use of language. 'Every Fatt must stand upon his own bottom' is the complacent response of Presumption who was fast asleep near the Cross, but 'a little out of the way'. One of his best known proverbial statements and apparently his own creation, is the one he gives to Christian regarding Talkative: 'His house is as empty of Religion, *as the white of an Egg is of savour*.' Throughout the work there is a flow of lovely natural proverbial expressions. In this characteristic Bunyan would undoubtedly please the poet Coleridge, who once said: 'Works of imagination should be written in a very plain language; the more purely imaginative they are the more necessary it is to be plain.'

Another aspect of Bunyan's language and style is the use of little rhymes to close stages of the journey or to suggest their significance. After he loses his burden at the Cross, Christian bursts into a rhymed song:

> *Thus far did I come loaden with my sin,*
> *Nor could ought ease the grief that I was in,*
> *Till I came hither: What a place is this!*

*Must here be the beginning of my bliss?*
*Must here the burden fall from off my back?*
*Must here the strings that bound it to me, crack?*
*Blest Cross! blest Sepulcher! blest rather be*
*The Man that there was put to shame for me.* (p. 32)

Little can be said for Bunyan as a poet, but scattered throughout the allegory are these little rhymes to point up or summarise an important episode. The same direct simplicity, characteristic of almost every page of his book, is a distinctive mark of his rhymes.

Whatever one may say or think of the way Bunyan made use of the direct, ordinary, proverbial and idiomatic speech of the working class, a reader must be equally aware of the near-lyrical prose he uses to describe Faithful rising from his ashes after being burned to death at the stake. Perhaps more convincing evidence that Bunyan can shift from the ordinary and the proverbial is found in his depiction of the glory of the Celestial City. He builds the emotional intensity through a series of splendid experiences for the pilgrims – such as the Delectable Mountains and Beulah – which lead up to the glorious moment of Christian's and Hopeful's reception into the Celestial City. Bunyan clearly reveals that these two pilgrims have travelled a long distance; they have made progress; they have come all of the turbulent way from the City of Destruction to the new Jerusalem. Shining angels are on the other side of the River to receive Christian and Hopeful. The King's musicians, clothed in white raiment, also await them. At the gate of the City, the pilgrims are arrayed in new clothes that shine like gold. They receive a crown on their heads; they hear harps play and bells ring. The Celestial City shines like the sun, the streets are paved with gold, and the angels sing 'without intermission, saying, "Holy, Holy, Holy, is the Lord".'

In this extraordinarily beautiful section, Bunyan shows the strong influence of the Bible on his style; it is also one of his most imaginative sections. And no study of Bunyan's language and style would be complete without specific reference to the influence of the King James Version of the Bible. Not only are there specific quotations from the Bible, but he alludes frequently to Biblical stories and weaves quotation and story into the substance of his own story. Equally biblical are the pictures of huge and undefined landscapes, and the sense of finality which they convey. It is not unusual to find Bunyan's language possessing the rhythm of the Hebrew poetry of the Old Testament.

If it is true, as some suggest, that Bunyan is following an old practice of preachers and religious writers in his language and style, it must also be added that his strong, controlled imagination takes his allegory far beyond much that had been done in religious writing. What Bunyan had to say in the seventeenth century was perhaps not entirely new; it was, however, his method of saying what he said that gave his era (and still offers to us) something very fresh.

Puns and *double entendres* pervade the second part. The arbour on the Hill Difficulty, for example, is a 'losing place', It is a 'losing place' for Christiana's bottle of 'spirits', as it had been for Christian's roll (his pardon) in Part One. Feeble-mind has suficient mind to request that upon his death his friends bury his feeble mind in a dung hill. Undoubtedly Bunyan intends a pun when, at the end of the looking-glass section, Mercy remarks to the shepherds of the Delectable Mountains: 'By this I know that I have obtained Favour in your Eyes.'

The pilgrims also find special delight in riddles, a technique that Bunyan now uses with considerable adroitness. Mr Great-heart, for example, tells Mr Honest the following riddle:

> He that will kill, must first be overcome:
> Who live abroad would, first must die at home.

Mr Honest wants Gaius to expound on the riddle, for he finds it to be 'a hard one', but Gaius replies that the riddle 'was put' to Honest and ' 'tis expected' that he solve it. Since there seems to be no escape for old Honest, he finally replies:

> He first by Grace must conquer'd be,
> That Sin would mortifie.
> And who, that lives, would convince me,
> Unto himself must die. (p. 220)

Gaius is obviously happy with Mr Honest's solution, for his quick response is: 'It is right . . . good Doctrine, and Experience teaches this.' On occasion Bunyan merges the riddle with the emblem, as he does in the Interpreter's House, which contains numerous emblematic pictures.

Songs and poems abound in the second part. As the pilgrims arrive at the Gate, the Keeper of the Gate has a trumpeter entertain the travellers. Minstrels provide dinner music at the Interpreter's House.

Bells and trumpets sound in Beulah. Certainly references to music
are more numerous in Part Two than in Part One. On rare occasions,
someone not travelling with the pilgrims offers a poem. One of the
finest is the shepherd boy's poem in the Valley of Humiliation, which
is included in the *Oxford Book of English Verse*:

> *He that is down, must fear no fall,*
> *He that is low, no Pride:*
> *He that is humble, ever shall*
> *Have God to be his Guide.*
>
> *I am content with what I have,*
> *Little be it, or much:*
> *And, Lord, Contentment still I crave,*
> *Because thou savest such.*
>
> *Fulness to such a burden is*
> *That go on Pilgrimage:*
> *Here little, and hereafter Bliss,*
> *Is best from Age to Age.* (p. 197)

Another well-known song, though altered in some hymn books, is
still sung today. This song, which belongs to Bunyan's Valiant-for-
truth, was sung at the funeral of the famous English political leader,
Sir Winston Churchill. Bunyan places the song following Valiant-for-
truth's declaration to Great-heart that he 'got into the way' by faith,
but he also adds that he 'fought all that set themselves against me'.
The words of the song are:

> *Who would true Valour see*
> *Let him come hither;*
> *One here will Constant be,*
> *Come Wind, come Weather.*
> *There's no* Discouragement,
> *Shall make him once* Relent,
> *His first avow'd* Intent,
> To be a Pilgrim.
>
> *Who so beset him round,*
> *With Dismal Storys,*

*Do but themselves Confound;*
*His Strength the more is.*
*No* Lyon *can him fright,*
*He'l with a* Gyant *Fight,*
*But he will have a right,*
To be a Pilgrim.

Hobgoblin, *nor foul* Fiend,
*Can* daunt *his Spirit:*
*He knows, he* at the end,
Shall Life Inherit.
*Then Fancies fly away,*
*He'l fear not what men say,*
*He'l labour Night and Day,*
To be a Pilgrim. (p. 247)

As some Bunyan scholars have observed, Part Two appears to promote church music. Although songs or poems pervade both Parts, they are usually present to make a spiritual point or to provide a transition from one episode to another. On occasion, they become small versions of an episode.

Proverbial statements are present on numerous pages of the Second Part. As in Part One, proverbs are further evidence of the manner in which Bunyan brings the language of prose narrative into his depiction of the human world, and he thinks it appropriate to have his characters use the common speech of ordinary men and women. Illustrative examples of this colourful speech are: 'One leak will sink a ship', 'as many Lives as a Cat', 'The wind is not always on our Backs', and scores of similar statements.

On occasion 'ordered set pieces' are among the literary features. The variations of an ordered pattern as each pilgrim receives a summons to cross the River of Death show a special excellence. There is the invitation, an emblematic token mostly drawn from the book of Ecclesiastes, the bequests of each pilgrim to friends, and his final words when crossing the river. Embodied in this rather lengthy section is a masterful depiction of the glory of Christian belief.

As allegory is the literary form of Part One, so also is it the genre of the Second Part. Dreams-within-the-dream are also present in Part Two. Lengthy doctrinal discussions, embodied within the allegory of Part One, are not prevalent in the sequel. Great-heart did, of course, deliver at the Cross a discourse on pardon and on the deity and humanity of Christ, but when doctrine is obviously present, it is usually presented in a dramatic manner. The more dramatic handling is evident in Mercy's lack of a specific invitation to salvation such as Christiana received; yet Mercy may enter through the Wicket-gate because of Christ's sacrifice on the cross. His death makes available an invitation to all; no one is excluded. The narrator is far less visible in this allegory than in Part One. When he is visible, he appears to be far more detached than the narrator of the First Part.

Emblems of terror and despair are by no means primary literary tools in Part Two. Doubting Castle, for example, contains no horror for these pilgrims who can march on the castle, kill Diffidence and cut off the head of her husband, Giant Despair. Even death itself holds no terror for this mature Christian community. Readers recall the fears of Christian and his need for reassurance in Part One. In the Second Part Bunyan shows the courageous manner in which Christiana takes leave of her fellow pilgrims. Not one of the summoned pilgrims shows any despair; their mature and strong faith enabled them to meet death bravely. No pilgrim fails to get to the Celestial City, though Mr Ready-to-hault gets to the river bank on crutches, and Mr Despondency and his daughter Miss Much-afraid have to be rescued by Great-heart from Despair. But for Mr Valiant-for-truth and Mr Stand-fast, as for all the strong Christian pilgrims, death holds not the least threat or sting.

Overall, Part One of *The Pilgrim's Progress* focuses on an individual on his way from the City of Destruction to the Celestial City; Part Two emphasises the benefits of shared Christian experience among a group of Christian pilgrims.

# 8 SPECIMEN PASSAGE
# AND COMMENTARY

This Parlor, is the heart of a Man that was
never sanctified by the sweet Grace of the
Gospel: The *dust*, is his Original Sin, and
inward Corruptions that have defiled the whole
Man. He that began to sweep at first, is the
Law; but She that brought water, and did
sprinkle it, is the Gospel: Now, whereas thou
sawest that so soon as the first began to
sweep, the dust did so fly about, that the
Room by him could not be cleansed, but that
thou wast almost choaked therewith, this is to
shew thee, that the Law, instead of cleansing
the heart (by its working) from sin, doth revive, put strength into, and increase it in
the soul, even as it doth discover and forbid
it, for it doth not give power to subdue . . . .
I have Crucified him to my self afresh, I have
despised his Person, I have despised his
Righteousness, I have counted his Blood an
unholy thing, I have done despite to the
Spirit of Grace: Therefore I have shut myself
out of all the Promises; and there now remains
to me nothing but threatnings, dreadful
threatnings . . .
God hath denied me repentance; his Word gives
me no encouragement to believe; yea, himself
hath shut me up in this Iron Cage: nor can

all the men in the World let me out. O
Eternity! Eternity! how shall I grapple with
the misery that I must meet with in Eternity?
(pp. 25, 29)

The passage describing the Interpreter's House is an excellent illustration of the visionary quality and emblematic habit of Bunyan's mind. The form is an allegory within the main allegory. The Interpreter is undoubtedly the Person of the Holy Spirit, who shows the things of Christ by the ordinary and familiar objects of life – a man lights a candle and Christian follows from room to room. He quotes words of Scripture which give illumination and high spiritual meaning to common objects in the various rooms. What Christian sees are pictures and scenes in motion. The first picture is that of a man with eyes lifted to heaven, with the best of Books (the Bible) in his hands, with truth upon his lips, and the world behind his back. The significance of a sincere teacher of the Bible, ready to teach the truth, precedes the emblematic passage for this study.

To bring the specific passage into focus, we will take a brief look at the way Bunyan introduces it. Interpreter takes Christian by the hand and leads him into a 'very large parlour that was full of dust, because never swept . . .'. At the request of the Interpreter, a man begins to sweep and dust begins 'so abundantly to fly about' that Christian almost chokes. Then the Interpreter asks a girl to bring water and 'sprinkle the Room'. Immediately, the room could be swept and cleaned 'with pleasure'. But what is the meaning of this emblem of the dusty room?

This lengthy quotation seems to explain every detail and leave nothing to a reader's mind and imagination. But, does it? We should think on previous scenes and look closely at the images. The Interpreter's scene imaginatively captures the theology of the Law (as stated in the first five books of the Old Testament), which Bunyan represents in an earlier image as an impending danger (Mount Sinai). Here the image of sweeping – the cleaning – produces the opposite of what it intends – swirling dust. What a brilliant image of sin is dust. It accumulates in a room. Something must be done to get rid of it, but what? The broom, the Law, only stirs it about until it gets into the air one tries to breathe. It produces irritation and debris. Getting choked on dust is no cleansing. What Bunyan further brilliantly captures is that the mercy of the Gospel (the sprinkling of the room) has joined the justice of the Law. The Interpreter shows Christian the differences between a Christian in the Way and the dusty room. He is clean through grace, not choking on a gradual accumulation of sin.

Each room of the Interpreter's House contains emblematic scenes, all calling for interpretation. There is a room with two children, Patience and Passion; another room in which a man seeks to extinguish with water a fire burning against a wall; and finally, a dark room which contains a man in an iron cage. Passion is the selfish life, but Patience is a marvellous virtue which involves discipline and the denial of indulgences in its varied forms. A fire against the wall suggests the various agencies such as temptation and discouragement by which Satan (the man casting water upon the flame) seeks to extinguish the 'inner fires' of one's life. The wonderful fact is that the flame is not put out, and the secret is that Christ is at the back of the wall pouring grace into the soul.

There are yet other scenes, including the man with the muck-rake, the spider, living in a beautiful room, the garden, with all flowers growing and living harmoniously, and the fair-appearing tree, rotten at the heart. One of the most unforgettable scenes is that of the Man in the Iron Cage, completely cut off from Christ and Grace. Christian asks, '*Is there no hope but you must be kept in this Iron Cage of Despair?*' After the man replies, 'No, none at all', he continues in the words of the latter part of the quoted passage.

Students must remember that the Man in the Iron Cage is unwilling to accept the Way one 'must go'. He is a reprobate, and grace is indeed withheld from him. The horrible despair is a depiction of his condition; he has no part in God's promises. Unlike the plight of Christian and Hopeful in Doubting Castle whose misery is temporary, the Man in the Iron Cage knows no reprieve.

What is especially significant about this passage is the way in which it shows in miniature the work of Bunyan. It is a set of allegorical tableaux within the whole allegory; it shows Bunyan taking ordinary objects like dust, a broom, water, a parlour and a cage, and investing these with invisible and spiritual significance. Questions and answers which make up dialogue flood the story, and it is obvious that Bunyan believes in the power of metaphorical language as he directs his writing toward religious ends. It is, of course, true that the reader is still in dream time in the little allegory. By the end of the episode of the Interpreter's House, the attentive reader comes very near to believing that dream time is over and, as at the end of the entire allegory, we are back in the waking time of the realistic present, both Bunyan's and ours. Without question, just as he leaves the burden of proof and action of the dream to readers at the end of *The Pilgrim's Progress*, so also to a great extent he does at this point, after filling the memory with pictures from the Interpreter's House.

# 9 CRITICAL RECEPTION

*The Pilgrim's Progress*, first published in 1678 in London by Nathaniel Ponder, had an immediate popular success. Two editions were sold out the first year. The third edition appeared in 1679 with notable additions which make this edition of Part One an almost complete version of the allegory as we know it.

The century following the publication of *The Pilgrim's Progress* offers varying viewpoints from authors and critics. Joseph Addison cited Bunyan as proof that even despicable writers had their admirers. William Cowper praised Bunyan and later apologised in refusing to name the recipient of his tribute, 'lest so despised a name/should move a sneer at thy deserved fame'. Other eighteenth-century authors and critics unabashedly praised Bunyan's work.

Jonathan Swift stated that he had been entertained and more confirmed by a few pages in *The Pilgrim's Progress* than by a long discussion on the will and intellect. In 1830 Robert Southey published an edition of *The Pilgrim's Progress* and clearly registered the fact that men of letters accepted Bunyan as a literary man.

Another nineteenth-century man of letters, Samuel Coleridge, contended that *The Pilgrim's Progress* was one of the few books that might be read repeatedly with always a new and different pleasure. Joining in the tribute to Bunyan, George Eliot, another nineteenth-century writer, stated that she was 'profoundly struck with the true genius manifested in the simple, vigorous, rhythmic style'.

In the first quarter of the twentieth century, J.W. MacKail wrote that his contemporaries approached *The Pilgrim's Progress*, not so much for edification or for the sake of its religious and ethical doctrines, as for 'its narrative and dramatic excellence, its unsurpassed power of characterization, its humour, its mastery of terse and lucid English'. Also in the twentieth century, Charles Angell Bradford declares that 'the allegory of allegories of the English-speaking race is Bunyan's *The Pilgrim's Progress*'.

Clifford Kent Wright applauds the raciness of its narrative and the graphic reality of the characters. C. S. Lewis praises the manner in which Bunyan opens the work with 'a picture which prints itself upon the eye like a flash of lightning'. For Lewis, the journey of the pilgrims is 'as enchanting as any in romance'. Angus Fletcher likes the 'emotive ambivalence' of allegory, and places Bunyan's name along with Swift, Melville and Kafka as writers who show ambivalence. What Fletcher basically has in mind is the ability of these writers to show the coexistence of opposite or conflicting feelings about a person or a situation. F. R. Leavis believes that creative power is 'compellingly' present in *The Pilgrim's Progress*.

What is also of special interest today is the enormous number of excellent studies being written on the works of John Bunyan. Fine scholarly editions of his allegory, and other writings, are published or are in the process of being published. His works are the focus of an extraordinary number of critical studies from contemporary scholars. All this interest should not lead us to believe that all studies heap lavish praise upon John Bunyan's allegory. This is never true for a literary author. What we do see is a recognition that *The Pilgrim's Progress* is an allegory, working out in human terms, dramatically and symbolically, Bunyan's portrayal of life in relation to man and to God. There is further recognition that Bunyan's work requires exactly what every good piece of imaginative literature requires: full and complete concentration.

# REVISION QUESTIONS

1. 'The story of *The Pilgrim's Progress* is a continuous metaphor.' Show why this statement is valid.

2. A reader rarely finds Bunyan's villains to be evil, but one does find them to be smug or snobbish, arrogant or stubborn. Think through the allegory and cite examples.

3. 'The Christian pilgrims are not always rare exemplars of faith and saintliness.' Show instances that support this statement.

4. Demonstrate the ways in which Bunyan captures the speech and mannerisms of selected characters.

5. Consider the order of the various temptations that Christian encounters on his journey from earth to heaven. Does there appear to be any special significance to the sequence?

6. Two thirds of the way through the allegory, Christian receives a stern command not to sleep on the Enchanted Ground. On this occasion the narrator is jolted awake, even though he subsequently resumes sleep. Explain the significance of his awaking, only to resume sleep.

7. The narrative structure of *The Pilgrim's Progress* depicts a coherent view of the progress of human life to a new and blessed state. Show how each episode and incident supports the allegorical scheme of the larger structure. Do the separate episodes constitute small allegories?

8. Select an episode and show how Bunyan uses language to make the episode vivid and lively.

9. What values may *The Pilgrim's Progress* have for the contemporary reader – even for the reader who does not accept Bunyan's religious convictions?

10. It is probable that few literary works have been as widely known, both to the educated and uneducated, as *The Pilgrim's Progress*. How do you account for the nature and degree of the success?

11. What evidence is there that Bunyan places more emphasis on the 'community of believers' in the Second Part than in Part One?

12. Show as many differences as you are able to find between the Second Part and Part One.

13. What purposes do the poems or songs serve in the Second Part?

14. Some readers claim that, in order to paint his characters, Bunyan concentrates on what they say, not on externals. Study several of the characters of the Second Part and draw your conclusions on Bunyan's method of characterisation.

15. Does the close of Part Two of the book seem effective? Give specific reasons for your response to this question.

16. What does Bunyan accomplish by writing the sequel to *The Pilgrim's Progress*? Again, be specific in your answer.

# FURTHER READING

**Primary sources**

N. H. Keeble (ed.), *John Bunyan, The Pilgrim's Progress*, The World's Classics (Oxford University Press, 1976).

J. Blanton Wharey (ed.), *The Pilgrim's Progress*, 2nd edn revised by Roger Sharrock (The Clarendon Press, 1960).

*The Miscellaneous Works of John Bunyan* (Oxford University Press, 1976). Thirteen volumes projected.

**Secondary sources**

Charles W. Baird, *John Bunyan: A Study in Narrative Technique* (Kennikat Press, 1977).

Robert L. Greaves, *John Bunyan* (William B. Eerdmans Publishing Company, 1969).

G. B. Harrison, *John Bunyan, A Study in Personality* (J. M. Dent and Sons, 1928).

U. Milo Kaufmann, *The Pilgrim's Progress and Traditions in Puritan Meditation* (Yale University Press, 1966).

Vincent Newey (ed.), *The Pilgrim's Progress: Critical and Historical Views* (Liverpool University Press, 1980).

Maureen Quilligan, *The Language of Allegory* (Cornell University Press, 1979); pp. 121–31 are especially helpful.

Lynn Veach Sadler, *John Bunyan* (Twayne Publishers, 1979).

Roger Sharrock, *Bunyan: The Pilgrim's Progress,* Casebook Series (Macmillan, 1976).

Henri Talon, *John Bunyan: The Man and His Work*, trans. Mrs Bernard Wall (Harvard University Press, 1951).

## Mastering English Literature

### Richard Gill

*Mastering English Literature* will help readers both to enjoy English Literature and to be successful in 'O' levels, 'A' levels and other public exams. It is an introduction to the study of poetry, novels and drama which helps the reader in four ways – by providing ways of approaching literature, by giving examples and practice exercises, by offering hints on how to write about literature, and by the author's own evident enthusiasm for the subject. With extracts from more than 200 texts, this is an enjoyable account of how to get the maximum satisfaction out of reading, whether it be for formal examinations or simply for pleasure.

## Work Out English Literature ('A' level)

### S.H. Burton

This book familiarises 'A' level English Literature candidates with every kind of test which they are likely to encounter. Suggested answers are worked out step by step and accompanied by full author's commentary. The book helps students to clarify their aims and establish techniques and standards so that they can make appropriate responses to similar questions when the examination pressures are on. It opens up fresh ways of looking at the full range of set texts, authors and critical judgements and motivates students to know more of these matters.

# Also from Macmillan

## CASEBOOK SERIES

The Macmillan *Casebook* series brings together the best of modern criticism with a selection of early reviews and comments. Each Casebook charts the development of opinion on a play, poem, or novel, or on a literary genre, from its first appearance to the present day.

## GENERAL THEMES

COMEDY: DEVELOPMENTS IN CRITICISM
D. J. Palmer

DRAMA CRITICISM: DEVELOPMENTS SINCE IBSEN
A. J. Hinchliffe

THE ENGLISH NOVEL: DEVELOPMENTS IN CRITICISM SINCE HENRY JAMES
Stephen Hazell

THE LANGUAGE OF LITERATURE
N. Page

THE PASTORAL MODE
Bryan Loughrey

THE ROMANTIC IMAGINATION
J. S. Hill

TRAGEDY: DEVELOPMENTS IN CRITICISM
R. P. Draper

## POETRY

WILLIAM BLAKE: SONGS OF INNOCENCE AND EXPERIENCE
Margaret Bottrall

BROWNING: MEN AND WOMEN AND OTHER POEMS
J. R. Watson

BYRON: CHILDE HAROLD'S PILGRIMAGE AND DON JUAN
John Jump

CHAUCER: THE CANTERBURY TALES
J. J. Anderson

COLERIDGE: THE ANCIENT MARINER AND OTHER POEMS
A. R. Jones and W. Tydeman

DONNE: SONGS AND SONETS
Julian Lovelock

T. S. ELIOT: FOUR QUARTETS
Bernard Bergonzi

T. S. ELIOT: PRUFROCK, GERONTION, ASH WEDNESDAY AND OTHER POEMS
B. C. Southam

T. S. ELIOT: THE WASTELAND
C. B. Cox and A. J. Hinchliffe

ELIZABETHAN POETRY: LYRICAL AND NARRATIVE
Gerald Hammond

THOMAS HARDY: POEMS
J. Gibson and T. Johnson

GERALD MANLEY HOPKINS: POEMS
Margaret Bottrall

KEATS: ODES
G. S. Fraser

KEATS: THE NARRATIVE POEMS
J. S. Hill

MARVELL: POEMS
Arthur Pollard

THE METAPHYSICAL POETS
Gerald Hammond

MILTON: PARADISE LOST
A. E. Dyson and Julian Lovelock

POETRY OF THE FIRST WORLD WAR
Dominic Hibberd

ALEXANDER POPE: THE RAPE OF THE LOCK
John Dixon Hunt

SHELLEY: SHORTER POEMS & LYRICS
Patrick Swinden

SPENSER: THE FAERIE QUEEN
Peter Bayley

TENNYSON: IN MEMORIAM
John Dixon Hunt

THIRTIES POETS: 'THE AUDEN GROUP'
Ronald Carter

WORDSWORTH: LYRICAL BALLADS
A. R. Jones and W. Tydeman

WORDSWORTH: THE PRELUDE
W. J. Harvey and R. Gravil

W. B. YEATS: POEMS 1919–1935
E. Cullingford

W. B. YEATS: LAST POEMS
Jon Stallworthy

# THE NOVEL AND PROSE

JANE AUSTEN: EMMA
David Lodge

JANE AUSTEN: NORTHANGER ABBEY AND PERSUASION
B. C. Southam

JANE AUSTEN: SENSE AND SENSIBILITY, PRIDE AND PREJUDICE AND MANSFIELD PARK
B. C. Southam

CHARLOTTE BRONTË: JANE EYRE AND VILLETTE
Miriam Allott

EMILY BRONTË: WUTHERING HEIGHTS
Miriam Allott

BUNYAN: THE PILGRIM'S PROGRESS
R. Sharrock

CONRAD: HEART OF DARKNESS, NOSTROMO AND UNDER WESTERN EYES
C. B. Cox

CONRAD: THE SECRET AGENT
Ian Watt

CHARLES DICKENS: BLEAK HOUSE
A. E. Dyson

CHARLES DICKENS: DOMBEY AND SON AND LITTLE DORRITT
Alan Shelston

CHARLES DICKENS: HARD TIMES, GREAT EXPECTATIONS AND OUR MUTUAL FRIEND
N. Page

GEORGE ELIOT: MIDDLEMARCH
Patrick Swinden

GEORGE ELIOT: THE MILL ON THE FLOSS AND SILAS MARNER
R. P. Draper

HENRY FIELDING: TOM JONES
Neil Compton

E. M. FORSTER: A PASSAGE TO INDIA
Malcolm Bradbury

HARDY: THE TRAGIC NOVELS
R. P. Draper

HENRY JAMES: WASHINGTON SQUARE AND THE PORTRAIT OF A LADY
Alan Shelston

JAMES JOYCE: DUBLINERS AND A PORTRAIT OF THE ARTIST AS A YOUNG MAN
Morris Beja

D. H. LAWRENCE: THE RAINBOW AND WOMEN IN LOVE
Colin Clarke

D. H. LAWRENCE: SONS AND LOVERS
Gamini Salgado

SWIFT: GULLIVER'S TRAVELS
Richard Gravil

THACKERAY: VANITY FAIR
Arthur Pollard

TROLLOPE: THE BARSETSHIRE
NOVELS
T. Bareham

VIRGINIA WOOLF: TO THE
LIGHTHOUSE
Morris Beja

# DRAMA

CONGREVE: COMEDIES
Patrick Lyons

T. S. ELIOT: PLAYS
Arnold P. Hinchliffe

JONSON: EVERY MAN IN HIS
HUMOUR AND THE ALCHEMIST
R. V. Holdsworth

JONSON: VOLPONE
J. A. Barish

MARLOWE: DR FAUSTUS
John Jump

MARLOWE: TAMBURLAINE,
EDWARD II AND THE JEW OF
MALTA
John Russell Brown

MEDIEVAL ENGLISH DRAMA
Peter Happé

O'CASEY: JUNO AND THE
PAYCOCK, THE PLOUGH AND THE
STARS AND THE SHADOW OF A
GUNMAN
R. Ayling

JOHN OSBORNE: LOOK BACK IN
ANGER
John Russell Taylor

WEBSTER: THE WHITE DEVIL AND
THE DUCHESS OF MALFI
R. V. Holdsworth

WILDE: COMEDIES
W. Tydeman

# SHAKESPEARE

SHAKESPEARE: ANTONY AND
CLEOPATRA
John Russell Brown

SHAKESPEARE: CORIOLANUS
B. A. Brockman

SHAKESPEARE: HAMLET
John Jump

SHAKESPEARE: HENRY IV PARTS
I AND II
G. K. Hunter

SHAKESPEARE: HENRY V
Michael Quinn

SHAKESPEARE: JULIUS CAESAR
Peter Ure

SHAKESPEARE: KING LEAR
Frank Kermode

SHAKESPEARE: MACBETH
John Wain

SHAKESPEARE: MEASURE FOR
MEASURE
G. K. Stead

SHAKESPEARE: THE MERCHANT
OF VENICE
John Wilders

SHAKESPEARE: A MIDSUMMER
NIGHT'S DREAM
A. W. Price

SHAKESPEARE: MUCH ADO
ABOUT NOTHING AND AS YOU
LIKE IT
John Russell Brown

SHAKESPEARE: OTHELLO
John Wain

SHAKESPEARE: RICHARD II
N. Brooke

SHAKESPEARE: THE SONNETS
Peter Jones

SHAKESPEARE: THE TEMPEST
D. J. Palmer

SHAKESPEARE: TROILUS AND
CRESSIDA
Priscilla Martin

SHAKESPEARE: TWELFTH NIGHT
D. J. Palmer

SHAKESPEARE: THE WINTER'S
TALE
Kenneth Muir

# MACMILLAN SHAKESPEARE VIDEO WORKSHOPS

## DAVID WHITWORTH

Three unique book and video packages, each examining a particular aspect of Shakespeare's work; tragedy, comedy and the Roman plays. Designed for all students of Shakespeare, each package assumes no previous knowledge of the plays and can serve as a useful introduction to Shakespeare for 'O' and 'A' level candidates as well as for students at colleges and institutes of further, higher and adult education.

The material is based on the New Shakespeare Company Workshops at the Roundhouse, adapted and extended for television. By combining the resources of television and a small theatre company, this exploration of Shakespeare's plays offers insights into varied interpretations, presentation, styles of acting as well as useful background information.

While being no substitute for seeing the whole plays in performance, it is envisaged that these video cassettes will impart something of the original excitement of the theatrical experience, and serve as a welcome complement to textual analysis leading to an enriched and broader view of the plays.

Each package consists of:

* the Macmillan Shakespeare editions of the plays concerned;

* a video cassette available in VHS or Beta;

* a leaflet of teacher's notes.

### THE TORTURED MIND
looks at the four tragedies Hamlet, Othello, Macbeth and King Lear.

### THE COMIC SPIRIT
examines the comedies Much Ado About Nothing, Twelfth Night, A Midsummer Night's Dream, and As You Like It.

### THE ROMAN PLAYS
Features Julius Caesar, Antony and Cleopatra and Coriolanus